The Wiley COBOL Syntax Reference Guide: With IBM and VAX Enhancements

Prepared by

NANCY STERN and ROBERT A. STERN

COBOL Syntax Reference Guide

I. COBOL Character Set

The following lists are in ascending order:

EBCDIC		ASCII	
	space		space
.	period, decimal point	"	quotation mark
<	less than	$	dollar sign
(	left parenthesis	'	single quotation mark
+	plus symbol	(	left parenthesis
$	dollar sign	)	right parenthesis

*	asterisk, multiplication		*	asterisk, multiplication
)	right parenthesis		+	plus symbol
;	semicolon		,	comma
-	hyphen, minus sign		-	hyphen, minus sign
/	slash, division		.	period, decimal point
,	comma		/	slash, division
>	greater than		0–9	digits
'	single quotation mark		;	semicolon
=	equal sign		<	less than
"	quotation mark		=	equal sign
a–z	lowercase letters		>	greater than
A–Z	uppercase letters		A–Z	uppercase letters
0–9	digits		a–z	lowercase letters

II. COBOL Reserved Words

Each COBOL compiler has a list of reserved words that:

1. Includes all entries in the ANS COBOL standard.
2. Includes additional entries not part of the standard but that are either VAX or IBM compiler extensions. These are called enhancements.

The following is based on the 1974 and 1985 American National Standard. You may find that your computer has additional reserved words. Diagnostic messages will print if you are using a reserved word incorrectly.

New reserved words that are not relevant for COBOL 74, but are relevant only for COBOL 85, are denoted with a single asterisk (∗). COBOL 74 reserved words that are *not* reserved in the new standard are denoted with a double asterisk (∗∗). Words in red are VAX COBOL 85 extensions. Words in blue are IBM COBOL 85 extensions. Boxed words are both VAX and IBM COBOL 85 extensions.

ACCEPT	CHARACTERS
ACCESS	CLASS ∗
ACTUAL	CLOCK-UNITS
ADD	CLOSE
ADVANCING	COBOL
AFTER	CODE
ALL	CODE-SET
ALLOWING	COLLATING
ALPHABET ∗	COLUMN
ALPHABETIC	COM-REG
ALPHABETIC-LOWER ∗	COMMA
ALPHABETIC-UPPER ∗	COMMIT
ALPHANUMERIC ∗	COMMON
ALPHANUMERIC-EDITED ∗	COMMUNICATION
ALSO	COMP
ALTER	COMP-1
ALTERNATE	COMP-2
AND	COMP-3
ANY ∗	COMP-4
APPLY	COMP-5
ARE	COMP-6
AREA	COMPUTATIONAL

AREAS
ASCENDING.
ASSIGN
AT
AUTHOR
AUTOTERMINATE

BASIS
BATCH
BEFORE
BEGINNING
BELL
BINARY *
BIT
BITS
BLANK
BLINKING
BLOCK
BOLD
BOOLEAN
BOTTOM
BY

CALL
CANCEL
CBL
CD
CF
CH
CHARACTER

COMPUTATIONAL-1
COMPUTATIONAL-2
COMPUTATIONAL-3
COMPUTATIONAL-4
COMPUTATIONAL-5
COMPUTATIONAL-6
COMPUTE
CONCURRENT
CONFIGURATION
CONNECT
CONSOLE
CONTAIN
CONTAINS
CONTENT *
CONTINUE *
CONTROL
CONTROLS
CONVERSION
CONVERTING *
COPY
CORE-INDEX
CORR
CORRESPONDING
COUNT
CURRENCY
CURRENT
CURRENT-DATE

DATA
DATE

4

DATE-COMPILED
DATE-WRITTEN
DAY
DAY-OF-WEEK *
DB
DB-ACCESS-CONTROL-KEY
DB-CONDITION
DB-CURRENT-RECORD-ID
DB-CURRENT-RECORD-NAME
DB-EXCEPTION
DBKEY
DB-KEY
DB-RECORD-NAME
DB-SET-NAME
DB-STATUS
DEBUG-SUB
DB-UWA
DE
DEBUG-CONTENTS
DEBUG-ITEM
DEBUG-LENGTH
DEBUG-LINE
DEBUG-NAME
DEBUG-NUMERIC-CONTENTS
DEBUG-SIZE
DEBUG-START
DEBUG-SUB
DEBUG-SUB-1
DEBUG-SUB-2
DEBUG-SUB-3

ECHO
EGCS
EGI
EJECT
ELSE
EMI
EMPTY
ENABLE
END
END-ACCEPT
END-ADD *
END-CALL *
END-COMMIT
END-COMPUTE *
END-CONNECT
END-DELETE *
END-DISCONNECT
END-DIVIDE *
END-ERASE
END-EVALUATE *
END-FETCH
END-FIND
END-FINISH
END-FREE
END-GET
END-IF *
ENDING
END-KEEP
END-MODIFY
END-MULTIPLY *

DEBUG-SUB-ITEM	END-OF-PAGE
DEBUG-SUB-N	END-PERFORM *
DEBUG-SUM-NUM	END-READ *
DEBUGGING	END-READY
DECIMAL-POINT	END-RECEIVE *
DECLARATIVES	END-RECONNECT
DEFAULT	END-RETURN *
DELETE	END-REWRITE *
DELIMITED	END-ROLLBACK
DELIMITER	END-SEARCH *
DEPENDING	END-START *
DESCENDING	END-STORE
DESCRIPTOR	END-STRING *
DESTINATION	END-SUBTRACT *
DETAIL	END-UNSTRING *
DICTIONARY	END-WRITE *
DISABLE	ENTER
DISCONNECT	ENTRY
DISP	ENVIRONMENT
DISPLAY	EOP
DISPLAY-1	EQUAL
DISPLAY-6	EQUALS
DISPLAY-7	ERASE
DISPLAY-9	ERROR
DIVIDE	ESI
DIVISION	EVALUATE *
DOES	EVERY **
DOWN	EXCEEDS
DUPLICATE	EXCEPTION
DUPLICATES	EXCLUSIVE
DYNAMIC	EXIT

6

EXOR
EXTEND
EXTERNAL *

FAILURE
FALSE *
FD
FETCH
FILE
FILE-CONTROL
FILE-LIMIT
FILE-LIMITS
FILLER
FINAL
FIND
FINISH
FIRST
FOOTING
FOR
FREE
FROM

GENERATE
GET
GIVING
GLOBAL *
GO
GOBACK
GREATER
GROUP

KEEP
KEY

LABEL
LAST
LD
LEADING
LEAVE
LEFT
LENGTH
LESS
LIMIT
LIMITS
LINAGE
LINAGE-COUNTER
LINE
LINE-COUNTER
LINES
LINKAGE
LOCALLY
LOCK
LOW-VALUE
LOW-VALUES

MATCH
MATCHES
MEMBER
MEMBERSHIP
MEMORY **
MERGE

HEADING	MESSAGE
HIGH-VALUE	MODE
HIGH-VALUES	MODIFY
	MODULES **
ID	MORE-LABELS
IDENTIFICATION	MOVE
IF	MULTIPLE
IN	MULTIPLY
INCLUDING	
INDEX	NATIVE
INDEXED	NEGATIVE
INDICATE	NEXT
INITIAL	NO
INITIALIZE *	NOMINAL
INITIATE	NON-NULL
INPUT	NONE
INPUT-OUTPUT	NOT
INSERT	NOTE
INSPECT	NULL
INSTALLATION	NULLS
INTO	NUMBER
INVALID	NUMERIC
I-O	NUMERIC-EDITED
I-O-CONTROL	
IS	OBJECT-COMPUTER
	OCCURS
JUST	OF
JUSTIFIED	OFF
	OFFSET
KANJI	OMITTED

ON
ONLY
OPEN
OPTIONAL
OR
ORDER *
ORGANIZATION
OTHER *
OTHERS
OUTPUT
OVERFLOW
OWNER

PACKED-DECIMAL *
PADDING *
PAGE
PAGE-COUNTER
PARAGRAPH
PASSWORD
PERFORM
PF
PH
PIC
PICTURE
PLUS
POINTER
POSITION
POSITIVE
PRESENT
PRINTING

REFERENCE-MODIFIER
REFERENCES
REGARDLESS
RELATIVE
RELEASE
RELOAD
REMAINDER
REMOVAL
RENAMES
REPLACE *
REPLACING
REPORT
REPORTING
REPORTS
REREAD
RERUN
RESERVE
RESET
RETAINING
RETRIEVAL
RETURN
RETURN-CODE
REVERSED
REWIND
REWRITE
RF
RH
RIGHT
RMS-FILENAME
RMS-STS

PRIOR
PROCEDURE
PROCEDURES
PROCEED
PROGRAM
PROGRAM-ID
PROTECTED
PURGE *

QUEUE
QUOTE
QUOTES

RANDOM
RD
READ
READERS
READY
REALM
REALMS
RECEIVE
RECONNECT
RECORD
RECORD-NAME
RECORD-OVERFLOW
RECORDING
RECORDS
REDEFINES
REEL
REFERENCE *

RMS-STV
ROLLBACK
ROUNDED
RUN

SAME
SCREEN
SD
SEARCH
SECTION
SECURITY
SEGMENT
SEGMENT-LIMIT
SELECT
SEND
SENTENCE
SEPARATE
SEQUENCE
SEQUENCE-NUMBER
SEQUENTIAL
SERVICE
SET
SETS
SHIFT-IN
SHIFT-OUT
SIGN
SIZE
SKIP-1
SKIP-2
SKIP-3

SORT	TOP
SORT-CONTROL	TRAILING
SORT-CORE-SIZE	TRUE *
SORT-FILE-SIZE	TYPE
SORT-MERGE	
SORT-MESSAGE	UNDERLINED
SORT-MODE-SIZE	UNEQUAL
SORT-RETURN	UNIT
SOURCE	UNLOCK
SOURCE-COMPUTER	UNSTRING
SPACE	UNTIL
SPACES	UP
SPECIAL-NAMES	UPDATE
STANDARD	UPDATERS
STANDARD-1 .	UPON
STANDARD-2 *	USAGE
START	USAGE-MODE
STATUS	USE
STOP	USING
STORE	
STRING	VALUE
SUB-QUEUE-1	VALUES
SUB-QUEUE-2	VARYING
SUB-QUEUE-3	
SUB-SCHEMA	WAIT
SUBTRACT	WHEN
SUCCESS	WHEN-COMPILED
SUM	WHERE
SUPPRESS	WITH
SYMBOLIC	WITHIN
SYNC	WORDS **

```
SYNCHRONIZED                    WORKING-STORAGE
                                WRITE
TABLE                           WRITE-ONLY
TALLY                           WRITERS
TALLYING
TAPE                            ZERO
TENANT                          ZEROES
TERMINAL                        ZEROS
TERMINATE
TEST                            +
TEXT                            -
THAN                            *
THEN *                          /
THROUGH                         **
THRU                            >
TIME                            <
TIME-OF-DAY                     =
TIMES                           >= *
TITLE                           <= *
TO
```

III. Complete COBOL Language Formats

This guide contains the composite language formats of the American National
Standard COBOL. Shaded entries are those that are applicable to COBOL 85
only. Entries in blue are IBM extensions. Entries in red are VAX extensions.
Entries with an * are both IBM and VAX extensions.

General Format for IDENTIFICATION DIVISION

$$\begin{Bmatrix} \underline{\text{IDENTIFICATION}} \ \underline{\text{DIVISION}}. \\ \underline{\text{ID}} \ \underline{\text{DIVISION}}. \end{Bmatrix}$$

PROGRAM-ID. program-name $\left[\text{IS} \begin{Bmatrix} \underline{\text{COMMON}} \\ \underline{\text{INITIAL}} \end{Bmatrix} \text{PROGRAM} \right]$.

[AUTHOR. [comment-entry] ...]
[INSTALLATION. [comment-entry] ...]
[DATE-WRITTEN. [comment-entry] ...]
[DATE-COMPILED. [comment-entry] ...]
[SECURITY. [comment-entry] ...]

General Format for ENVIRONMENT DIVISION*

[ENVIRONMENT DIVISION.
[CONFIGURATION SECTION.
[SOURCE-COMPUTER. [computer-name [WITH DEBUGGING MODE].]]
[OBJECT-COMPUTER. [computer-name
     [PROGRAM COLLATING SEQUENCE IS alphabet-name-1]
     [SEGMENT-LIMIT IS segment-number].]]

[SPECIAL-NAMES. [[implementor-name-1

$$\left\{\begin{array}{l}\text{IS mnemonic-name-1} \quad [\underline{ON}\ \text{STATUS IS condition-name-1}\ [\underline{OFF}\ \text{STATUS IS condition-name-2}]]\\ \text{IS mnemonic-name-2} \quad [\underline{OFF}\ \text{STATUS IS condition-name-2}\ [\underline{ON}\ \text{STATUS IS condition-name-1}]]\\ \underline{ON}\ \text{STATUS IS condition-name-1}\ [\underline{OFF}\ \text{STATUS IS condition-name-2}]\\ \underline{OFF}\ \text{STATUS IS condition-name-2}\ [\underline{ON}\ \text{STATUS IS condition-name-1}]\end{array}\right\} \Bigg]\ \ldots$$

[ALPHABET alphabet-name-1 IS

$$\left\{\begin{array}{l}\text{ASCII}\\ \text{EBCDIC/}\end{array}\right\}$$

$$\left\{\begin{array}{l}\text{STANDARD-1}\\ \text{STANDARD-2}\\ \text{NATIVE}\\ \text{implementor-name-2}\\ \left\{\text{literal-1}\left[\begin{array}{l}\left\{\begin{array}{l}\underline{THROUGH}\\ \underline{THRU}\end{array}\right\}\text{literal-2}\\ \{\underline{ALSO}\ \text{literal-3}\}\ \ldots\end{array}\right]\right\}\ \ldots\end{array}\right\}\ \ldots$$

$$\left[\underline{SYMBOLIC}\ \text{CHARACTERS}\left\{\{\text{symbolic-character-1}\}\ \ldots\ \left\{\begin{array}{l}\text{IS}\\ \text{ARE}\end{array}\right\}\{\text{integer-1}\}\ \ldots\right\}\ \ldots\right.$$

---

*The ENVIRONMENT DIVISION, CONFIGURATION SECTION, and INPUT-OUTPUT SECTION entries are required for COBOL 74.

14

$$\left[\underline{\text{IN}} \text{ alphabet-name-2}\right]\Big\}\Big] \ldots$$

$$\left[\underline{\text{CLASS}} \text{ class-name } \text{IS} \quad \left\{\text{literal-4} \quad \left[\left\{\frac{\underline{\text{THROUGH}}}{\underline{\text{THRU}}}\right\} \text{ literal-5}\right]\right\} \ldots \right] \ldots$$

```
[CURRENCY SIGN IS literal-6]
[DECIMAL-POINT IS COMMA].]]]
[INPUT-OUTPUT SECTION.
FILE-CONTROL.
    {file-control-entry} ...
[I-O-CONTROL.
```

$$\left[\left[\underline{\text{SAME}} \quad \begin{bmatrix}\underline{\text{RECORD}}\\ \underline{\text{SORT}}\\ \underline{\text{SORT-MERGE}}\end{bmatrix} \text{ AREA FOR file-name-1} \quad \text{\{file-name-2\}} \ldots \right] \ldots\right.$$

```
[MULTIPLE FILE TAPE CONTAINS
    {file-name-3 [POSITION integer-1] } ... ] ... .]]]]
```

General Format for FILE-CONTROL **Entry**

SEQUENTIAL FILE

SELECT [OPTIONAL] file-name-1

$$\underline{\text{ASSIGN}} \text{ TO} \quad \left\{ \begin{array}{l} \text{implementor-name-1} \\ \text{literal-1} \end{array} \right\} \dots$$

$$\left[\underline{\text{RESERVE}} \text{ integer-1} \quad \left[\begin{array}{l} \text{AREA} \\ \text{AREAS} \end{array} \right] \right]$$

[[ORGANIZATION IS] SEQUENTIAL]

$$\left[\underline{\text{BLOCK}} \text{ CONTAINS} \quad [\text{smallest-block } \underline{\text{TO}}] \quad \text{blocksize} \quad \left\{ \begin{array}{l} \text{RECORDS} \\ \text{CHARACTERS} \end{array} \right\} \right]$$

[CODE-SET IS   alpha-name]

$$\left[\underline{\text{PADDING}} \text{ CHARACTER IS} \quad \left\{ \begin{array}{l} \text{data-name-1} \\ \text{literal-2} \end{array} \right\} \right]$$

$$\left[\underline{\text{RECORD}} \underline{\text{DELIMITER}} \text{ IS} \quad \left\{ \begin{array}{l} \underline{\text{STANDARD-1}} \\ \text{implementor-name-2} \end{array} \right\} \right]$$

[ACCESS MODE IS SEQUENTIAL]
[FILE STATUS IS data-name-2].

RELATIVE FILE

$$\underline{\text{SELECT}} \quad [\text{OPTIONAL}] \quad \text{file-name-1}$$

$$\underline{\text{ASSIGN}} \text{ TO} \quad \left\{ \begin{array}{l} \text{implementor-name-1} \\ \text{literal-1} \end{array} \right\} \dots$$

$$\left[\underline{\text{RESERVE}} \text{ integer-1} \quad \left[\begin{array}{l} \text{AREA} \\ \text{AREAS} \end{array} \right] \right]$$

[ORGANIZATION IS] RELATIVE

$$\left[\text{BLOCK CONTAINS} \quad [\text{smallest-block } \underline{\text{TO}}] \quad \text{blocksize} \quad \left\{\begin{array}{l}\underline{\text{RECORDS}}\\ \text{CHARACTERS}\end{array}\right\}\right]$$

[PASSWORD IS data-name]

$$\left[\underline{\text{ACCESS}} \text{ MODE IS} \left\{\begin{array}{l}\underline{\text{SEQUENTIAL}} \quad [\underline{\text{RELATIVE}} \text{ KEY IS data-name-1}] \\ \left\{\begin{array}{l}\underline{\text{RANDOM}}\\ \underline{\text{DYNAMIC}}\end{array}\right\} \quad \underline{\text{RELATIVE}} \text{ KEY IS data-name-1}\end{array}\right\}\right]$$

[FILE STATUS IS data-name-2].

INDEXED FILE

SELECT [OPTIONAL] file-name-1

$$\underline{\text{ASSIGN}} \text{ TO} \left\{\begin{array}{l}\text{implementor-name-1}\\ \text{literal-1}\end{array}\right\} \ldots$$

$$\left[\underline{\text{RESERVE}} \text{ integer-1} \left[\begin{array}{l}\text{AREA}\\ \text{AREAS}\end{array}\right]\right]$$

[ORGANIZATION IS] INDEXED

$$\left[\underline{\text{BLOCK}} \text{ CONTAINS} \quad [\text{smallest-block } \underline{\text{TO}}] \quad \text{blocksize} \quad \left\{\begin{array}{l}\underline{\text{RECORDS}}\\ \text{CHARACTERS}\end{array}\right\}\right]$$

[PASSWORD IS data-name]

$$
\left[\underline{\text{ACCESS}} \text{ MODE IS } \left\{ \begin{array}{l} \underline{\text{SEQUENTIAL}} \\ \underline{\text{RANDOM}} \\ \underline{\text{DYNAMIC}} \end{array} \right\} \right]
$$

<u>RECORD</u> KEY IS data-name-1
[<u>ALTERNATE</u> <u>RECORD</u> KEY IS data-name-2 [WITH <u>DUPLICATES</u>]] ...
[FILE <u>STATUS</u> IS data-name-3].

SORT OR MERGE FILE

$$
\underline{\text{SELECT}} \text{ file-name-1} \quad \underline{\text{ASSIGN}} \text{ TO } \left\{ \begin{array}{l} \text{implementor-name-1} \\ \text{literal-1} \end{array} \right\} \cdots \quad .
$$

REPORT FILE

<u>SELECT</u> [<u>OPTIONAL</u>] file-name-1

$$
\underline{\text{ASSIGN}} \text{ TO } \left\{ \begin{array}{l} \text{implementor-name-1} \\ \text{literal-1} \end{array} \right\} \cdots
$$

$$
\left[\underline{\text{RESERVE}} \text{ integer-1} \left[\begin{array}{l} \text{AREA} \\ \text{AREAS} \end{array} \right] \right]
$$

[[<u>ORGANIZATION</u> IS] <u>SEQUENTIAL</u>]

$$
\left[\underline{\text{BLOCK}} \text{ CONTAINS } [\text{smallest-block } \underline{\text{TO}}] \text{ blocksize } \left\{ \begin{array}{l} \text{RECORDS} \\ \text{CHARACTERS} \end{array} \right\} \right]
$$

[<u>CODE-SET</u> IS alpha-name]

$$
\left[
\begin{array}{l}
\left[\underline{\text{PADDING}} \text{ CHARACTER IS } \left\{ \begin{array}{l} \text{data-name-1} \\ \text{literal-1} \end{array} \right\} \right] \\
\left[\underline{\text{RECORD}} \ \underline{\text{DELIMITER}} \text{ IS } \left\{ \begin{array}{l} \underline{\text{STANDARD-1}} \\ \text{implementor-name-2} \end{array} \right\} \right]
\end{array}
\right]
$$

$$
\left[\underline{\text{ACCESS}} \text{ MODE IS } \underline{\text{SEQUENTIAL}} \right]
$$

$$
\left[\text{FILE } \underline{\text{STATUS}} \text{ IS data-name-2} \right].
$$

General Format—`I-O-CONTROL`

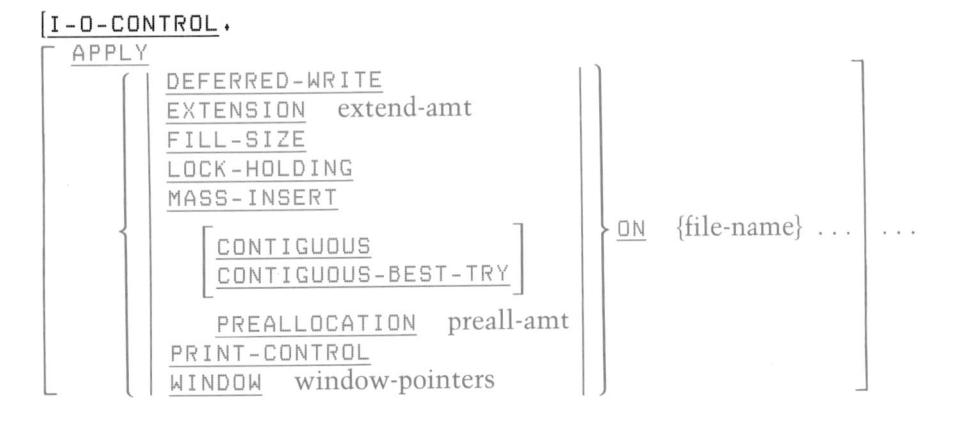

```
[I-O-CONTROL,
   APPLY
```

$$\left[\; \underline{\text{; RERUN}} \quad \left[\underline{\text{ON}} \quad \left\{\begin{matrix} \text{file-name-1} \\ \text{implementor-name} \end{matrix}\right\}\right]\right.$$

$$\left. \text{EVERY} \quad \left\{\begin{matrix} \left\{\begin{matrix} [\underline{\text{END}}\ \text{OF}] \quad \left\{\begin{matrix} \underline{\text{REEL}} \\ \underline{\text{UNIT}} \end{matrix}\right\} \\ \text{integer-1} \quad \underline{\text{RECORDS}} \end{matrix}\right\} \text{OF} \quad \text{file-name-2} \\ \text{integer-2} \quad \underline{\text{CLOCK-UNITS}} \\ \text{condition-name} \end{matrix}\right\}\right] \ldots$$

$$\left[\; \underline{\text{; SAME}} \quad \left[\begin{matrix} \underline{\text{RECORD}} \\ \underline{\text{SORT}} \\ \underline{\text{SORT-MERGE}} \end{matrix}\right] \text{AREA FOR} \quad \text{file-name-3} \quad \{, \text{file-name-4}\} \ldots \right] \ldots$$

[; <u>MULTIPLE FILE</u> TAPE CONTAINS file-name-5 [<u>POSITION</u> integer-3]

      [, file-name-6 [<u>POSITION</u> integer-4]] ...] ...]].

General Format for DATA DIVISION

[DATA DIVISION.
[SUB-SCHEMA SECTION. [subschema-entry [keeplist-entry] ...]]
[FILE SECTION.
[file-description-entry
{record-description-entry} ...] ...
[sort-merge-file-description-entry
{record-description-entry} ...] ...
[report-file-description-entry] ...]

[WORKING-STORAGE SECTION.

$$\begin{bmatrix} \text{77-level-description-entry} \\ \text{record-description-entry} \end{bmatrix} \; \cdots \; \Bigg]$$

[LINKAGE SECTION.

$$\begin{bmatrix} \text{77-level-description-entry} \\ \text{record-description-entry} \end{bmatrix} \; \cdots \; \Bigg]$$

[COMMUNICATION SECTION.
[communication-description-entry
[record-description-entry] ...] ...]
[REPORT SECTION.
[report-description-entry
{report-group-description-entry} ...] ...]]

General Format—Subschema Description

DB   subschema-name   WITHIN   schema-name

$$\left[\text{FOR} \quad \text{database-name} \right] \left[\begin{Bmatrix} \text{THRU} \\ \text{THROUGH} \end{Bmatrix} \quad \text{stream-name} \right]$$

General Format—Keeplist Description

LD   keeplist-name   [LIMIT IS   integer].

General Format for File Description Entry

SEQUENTIAL FILE

FD   file-name-1

    [IS EXTERNAL]
    [IS GLOBAL]

$$\left[\text{BLOCK CONTAINS } [\text{integer-1 TO}] \quad \text{integer-2} \left\{ \begin{array}{l} \text{RECORDS} \\ \text{CHARACTERS} \end{array} \right\} \right]$$

$$\left[\text{RECORD} \left\{ \begin{array}{l} \text{CONTAINS integer-3 CHARACTERS} \\ \text{IS VARYING IN SIZE [[FROM integer-4] [TO integer-5] CHARACTERS]} \\ \quad\quad [\text{DEPENDING ON data-name-1}] \\ \text{CONTAINS integer-6 TO integer-7 CHARACTERS} \end{array} \right\} \right]$$

$$\left[\text{LABEL} \left\{ \begin{array}{l} \text{RECORD IS} \\ \text{RECORDS ARE} \end{array} \right\} \left\{ \begin{array}{l} \text{STANDARD} \\ \text{OMITTED} \end{array} \right\} \right]$$

$$\left[\text{VALUE OF} \left\{ \text{implementor-name-1 IS} \left\{ \begin{array}{l} \text{data-name-2} \\ \text{literal-1} \end{array} \right\} \right\} \dots \right]$$

$$\left[\text{DATA} \left\{ \begin{array}{l} \text{RECORD IS} \\ \text{RECORDS ARE} \end{array} \right\} \{\text{data-name-3}\} \dots \right]$$

$$\left[\text{LINAGE IS} \left\{ \begin{array}{l} \text{data-name-4} \\ \text{integer-8} \end{array} \right\} \text{LINES} \left[\text{WITH FOOTING AT} \left\{ \begin{array}{l} \text{data-name-5} \\ \text{integer-9} \end{array} \right\} \right] \right.$$

$$\left. \left[\text{LINES AT TOP} \left\{ \begin{array}{l} \text{data-name-6} \\ \text{integer-10} \end{array} \right\} \right] \left[\text{LINES AT BOTTOM} \left\{ \begin{array}{l} \text{data-name-7} \\ \text{integer-11} \end{array} \right\} \right] \right]$$

22

[CODE-SET IS alphabet-name-1].
[[ACCESS MODE IS] SEQUENTIAL]
[FILE STATUS IS file-status].

RELATIVE FILE

FD file-name-1
   [IS EXTERNAL]
   [IS GLOBAL]

$$\left[\text{BLOCK CONTAINS } [\text{integer-1 } \underline{TO}] \text{ integer-2} \left\{ \begin{array}{l} \underline{\text{RECORDS}} \\ \text{CHARACTERS} \end{array} \right\} \right]$$

$$\left[\underline{\text{RECORD}} \left\{ \begin{array}{l} \text{CONTAINS integer-3 CHARACTERS} \\ \text{IS } \underline{\text{VARYING}} \text{ IN SIZE } [[\text{FROM integer-4}] [\underline{TO} \text{ integer-5}] \text{ CHARACTERS}] \\ \quad [\underline{\text{DEPENDING}} \text{ ON data-name-1}] \\ \text{CONTAINS integer-6 } \underline{TO} \text{ integer-7 CHARACTERS} \end{array} \right\} \right]$$

$$\left[\underline{\text{LABEL}} \left\{ \begin{array}{l} \underline{\text{RECORD}} \text{ IS} \\ \underline{\text{RECORDS}} \text{ ARE} \end{array} \right\} \left\{ \begin{array}{l} \underline{\text{STANDARD}} \\ \underline{\text{OMITTED}} \end{array} \right\} \right]$$

$$\left[\underline{\text{VALUE}} \ \underline{\text{OF}} \ \left\{ \text{implementor-name-1 IS} \left\{ \begin{array}{l} \text{data-name-2} \\ \text{literal-1} \end{array} \right\} \right\} \ \cdots \right]$$

$$\left[\underline{\text{DATA}} \left\{ \begin{array}{l} \underline{\text{RECORD}} \text{ IS} \\ \underline{\text{RECORDS}} \text{ ARE} \end{array} \right\} \ \{\text{data-name-3}\} \ \cdots \ \right].$$

$$\left[[\underline{\text{ACCESS}} \text{ MODE IS}] \left\{ \begin{array}{l} \underline{\text{SEQUENTIAL}} \ [\underline{\text{RELATIVE}} \text{ KEY IS rel-key}] \\ \left\{ \begin{array}{l} \underline{\text{RANDOM}} \\ \underline{\text{DYNAMIC}} \end{array} \right\} \ \underline{\text{RELATIVE}} \text{ KEY IS rel-key} \end{array} \right. \right]$$

[FILE <u>STATUS</u> IS file-status]

INDEXED FILE

<u>FD</u> file-name-1
   [IS <u>EXTERNAL</u>]
   [IS <u>GLOBAL</u>]

$$
\left[\ \underline{BLOCK}\ CONTAINS\ \ [integer\text{-}1\ \underline{TO}]\ \ integer\text{-}2\ \left\{ \begin{array}{l} RECORDS \\ CHARACTERS \end{array} \right\} \right]
$$

$$
\left[\ \underline{RECORD}\ \left\{ \begin{array}{l} CONTAINS\ integer\text{-}3\ CHARACTERS \\ IS\ \underline{VARYING}\ IN\ SIZE\ [[FROM\ integer\text{-}4]\ [\underline{TO}\ integer\text{-}5]\ CHARACTERS] \\ \quad\quad [\underline{DEPENDING}\ ON\ data\text{-}name\text{-}1] \\ CONTAINS\ integer\text{-}6\ \underline{TO}\ integer\text{-}7\ CHARACTERS \end{array} \right\} \right]
$$

$$
\left[\ \underline{LABEL}\ \left\{ \begin{array}{l} \underline{RECORD}\ IS \\ \underline{RECORDS}\ ARE \end{array} \right\} \left\{ \begin{array}{l} \underline{STANDARD} \\ \underline{OMITTED} \end{array} \right\} \right]
$$

$$
\left[\ \underline{VALUE}\ \underline{OF}\ \left\{ implementor\text{-}name\text{-}1\ \ IS\ \left\{ \begin{array}{l} data\text{-}name\text{-}2 \\ literal\text{-}1 \end{array} \right\} \right\} \ \dots \right]
$$

$$
\left[\ \underline{DATA}\ \left\{ \begin{array}{l} \underline{RECORD}\ IS \\ \underline{RECORDS}\ ARE \end{array} \right\} \ (data\text{-}name\text{-}3)\ \dots\ \right].
$$

$$
\left[\ [\underline{ACCESS}\ MODE\ IS]\ \left\{ \begin{array}{l} \underline{SEQUENTIAL} \\ \underline{RANDOM} \\ \underline{DYNAMIC} \end{array} \right\} \right]
$$

<u>RECORD</u> KEY IS rec-key
[<u>ALTERNATE</u> <u>RECORD</u> KEY IS alt-key [WITH <u>DUPLICATES</u>]] ...
[FILE <u>STATUS</u> IS file-status].

SORT-MERGE FILE

<u>SD</u> file-name-1

$$\left[\underline{RECORD} \left\{ \begin{array}{l} \texttt{CONTAINS integer-1 CHARACTERS} \\ \texttt{IS } \underline{\texttt{VARYING}} \texttt{ IN SIZE } [[\texttt{FROM integer-2] } [\underline{\texttt{TO}} \texttt{ integer-3] CHARACTERS}] \\ \quad [\underline{\texttt{DEPENDING}} \texttt{ ON data-name-1}] \\ \texttt{CONTAINS integer-4 } \underline{\texttt{TO}} \texttt{ integer-5 CHARACTERS} \end{array} \right\} \right]$$

$$\left[\underline{\texttt{DATA}} \left\{ \begin{array}{l} \underline{\texttt{RECORD}} \texttt{ IS} \\ \underline{\texttt{RECORDS}} \texttt{ ARE} \end{array} \right\} \quad \{\texttt{data-name-2}\} \ldots \right]$$

REPORT FILE

<u>FD</u> file-name-1

[IS <u>EXTERNAL</u>]

[IS <u>GLOBAL</u>]

$$\left[\underline{\texttt{BLOCK}} \texttt{ CONTAINS} \quad [\texttt{integer-1 } \underline{\texttt{TO}}] \quad \texttt{integer-2} \left\{ \begin{array}{l} \underline{\texttt{RECORDS}} \\ \texttt{CHARACTERS} \end{array} \right\} \right]$$

$$\left[\underline{RECORD} \left\{ \begin{array}{l} \texttt{CONTAINS integer-3 CHARACTERS} \\ \texttt{IS } \underline{\texttt{VARYING}} \texttt{ IN SIZE } [[\texttt{FROM integer-4] } [\underline{\texttt{TO}} \texttt{ integer-5] CHARACTERS}] \\ \quad [\underline{\texttt{DEPENDING}} \texttt{ ON data-name-1}] \\ \texttt{CONTAINS integer-6 } \underline{\texttt{TO}} \texttt{ integer-7 CHARACTERS} \end{array} \right\} \right]$$

$$\left[\underline{\texttt{LABEL}} \left\{ \begin{array}{l} \underline{\texttt{RECORD}} \texttt{ IS} \\ \underline{\texttt{RECORDS}} \texttt{ ARE} \end{array} \right\} \left\{ \begin{array}{l} \underline{\texttt{STANDARD}} \\ \underline{\texttt{OMITTED}} \end{array} \right\} \right]$$

$$\left[\underline{\texttt{VALUE}} \underline{\texttt{OF}} \left\{ \texttt{implementor-name-1 IS} \left\{ \begin{array}{l} \texttt{data-name-2} \\ \texttt{literal-1} \end{array} \right\} \right\} \ldots \right]$$

```
[[ACCESS MODE IS] SEQUENTIAL]
[CODE-SET IS alphabet-name-1]

⎧REPORT IS  ⎫
⎨           ⎬   {report-name-1} ...
⎩REPORTS ARE⎭

[FILE STATUS IS  file-status].
```

General Format for Data Description Entry

FORMAT 1

level-number   ⎡data-name-1⎤
               ⎣FILLER   ⎦

[REDEFINES data-name-2]
[IS EXTERNAL]
[IS GLOBAL]

⎡⎧PICTURE⎫   ⎤
⎢⎨   ⎬   IS character-string⎥
⎣⎩PIC   ⎭   ⎦

```
       ┌                          ┐
       │          ╭ BINARY          ╮│
       │          │ COMPUTATIONAL-1* ││
       │          │ COMP-1*          ││
       │          │ COMPUTATIONAL-2* ││
       │          │ COMP-2*          ││
       │ [USAGE IS]│ COMPUTATIONAL-3* ││
       │          │ COMP-3*          ││
       │          │ DISPLAY          ││
       │          │ DISPLAY-1*       ││
       │          │ INDEX            ││
       │          │ PACKED-DECIMAL   ││
       │          ╰ POINTER*         ╯│
       └                          ┘
```

```
┌                                                    ┐
│ [SIGN IS]  ╭ LEADING  ╮  [SEPARATE CHARACTER]      │
│            ╰ TRAILING ╯                            │
└                                                    ┘
```

```
┌                                                                   ┐
│ OCCURS integer-2 TIMES                                            │
│         ┌ ╭ ASCENDING  ╮                            ┐             │
│         │ ╰ DESCENDING ╯  KEY IS   {data-name-3} ... │ ...         │
│                                                                   │
│         [INDEXED BY   {index-name-1} ... ]                       │
│ OCCURS integer-1 TO integer-2 TIMES DEPENDING ON data-name-4      │
│         ┌ ╭ ASCENDING  ╮                            ┐             │
│         │ ╰ DESCENDING ╯  KEY IS   {data-name-3} ... │ ...         │
│                                                                   │
│         [INDEXED BY   {index-name-1} ... ]                       │
└                                                                   ┘
```

$$\left[\left[\begin{Bmatrix} \underline{\text{SYNCHRONIZED}} \\ \underline{\text{SYNC}} \end{Bmatrix} \quad \begin{bmatrix} \underline{\text{LEFT}} \\ \underline{\text{RIGHT}} \end{bmatrix}\right]\right]$$

$$\left[\begin{Bmatrix} \underline{\text{JUSTIFIED}} \\ \underline{\text{JUST}} \end{Bmatrix} \quad \text{RIGHT}\right]$$

$$\left[\underline{\text{BLANK}} \text{ WHEN } \begin{Bmatrix} \underline{\text{ZERO}} \\ \text{ZEROES} \\ \text{ZEROS} \end{Bmatrix}\right]$$

$$\left[\underline{\text{VALUE}} \text{ IS } \begin{Bmatrix} \text{literal-1} \\ \underline{\text{EXTERNAL}} \quad \text{external-name} \\ \underline{\text{REFERENCE}} \quad \text{data-name} \\ \text{NULL} \\ \text{NULLS} \end{Bmatrix}\right].$$

FORMAT 2

$$66 \quad \text{data-name-1} \;\underline{\text{RENAMES}}\; \text{data-name-2} \quad \left[\begin{Bmatrix} \underline{\text{THROUGH}} \\ \underline{\text{THRU}} \end{Bmatrix} \quad \text{data-name-3}\right].$$

FORMAT 3

88 condition-name-1 $\begin{Bmatrix} \underline{\text{VALUE}} \text{ IS} \\ \underline{\text{VALUES}} \text{ ARE} \end{Bmatrix}$ $\left\{ \begin{matrix} \begin{Bmatrix} \text{literal-1} \\ \underline{\text{EXTERNAL}} \quad \text{external-name} \\ \underline{\text{REFERENCE}} \quad \text{data-name} \\ \text{low-val} \end{Bmatrix} \\ \left[\begin{Bmatrix} \underline{\text{THROUGH}} \\ \underline{\text{THRU}} \end{Bmatrix} \begin{Bmatrix} \text{literal-2} \\ \underline{\text{EXTERNAL}} \quad \text{external-name} \\ \underline{\text{REFERENCE}} \quad \text{data-name} \\ \text{high-val} \end{Bmatrix} \right] \end{matrix} \right\} \dots$

General Format for Communication Description Entry

FORMAT 1

CD   cd-name-1

```
                       ⎡[[SYMBOLIC QUEUE IS data-name-1]                    ⎤
                       ⎢     [SYMBOLIC SUB-QUEUE-1 IS data-name-2]          ⎥
                       ⎢     [SYMBOLIC SUB-QUEUE-2 IS data-name-3]          ⎥
                       ⎢     [SYMBOLIC SUB-QUEUE-3 IS data-name-4]          ⎥
                       ⎢     [MESSAGE DATE IS data-name-5]                  ⎥
                       ⎢     [MESSAGE TIME IS data-name-6]                  ⎥
      FOR [INITIAL] INPUT    [SYMBOLIC SOURCE IS data-name-7]
                       ⎢     [TEXT LENGTH IS data-name-8]                   ⎥
                       ⎢     [END KEY IS data-name-9]                       ⎥
                       ⎢     [STATUS KEY IS data-name-10]                   ⎥
                       ⎢     [MESSAGE COUNT IS data-name-11]]               ⎥
                       ⎢[data-name-1, data-name-2, data-name-3,            ⎥
                       ⎢     data-name-4, data-name-5, data-name-6,         ⎥
                       ⎢     data-name-7, data-name-8, data-name-9,         ⎥
                       ⎣     data-name-10, data-name-11]                    ⎦
```

FORMAT 2

CD cd-name-1 FOR OUTPUT
    [DESTINATION COUNT IS data-name-1]
    [TEXT LENGTH IS data-name-2]
    [STATUS KEY IS data-name-3]
    [DESTINATION TABLE OCCURS integer-1 TIMES
        [INDEXED BY {index-name-1} ...]]
    [ERROR KEY IS data-name-4]
    [SYMBOLIC DESTINATION IS data-name-5].

FORMAT 3

CD cd-name-1

```
                  ┌ [[MESSAGE DATE IS data-name-1]                     ┐
                  │   [MESSAGE TIME IS data-name-2]                     │
                  │   [SYMBOLIC TERMINAL IS data-name-3]                │
FOR [INITIAL] I-O │   [TEXT LENGTH IS data-name-4]                     │
                  │   [END KEY IS data-name-5]                          │
                  │   [STATUS KEY IS data-name-6]]                      │
                  │ [data-name-1, data-name-2, data-name-3,            │
                  └    data-name-4, data-name-5, data-name-6]          ┘
```

General Format for Report Description Entry

RD report-name-1
    [IS GLOBAL]
    [CODE literal-1]

$$\left[\left\{ \begin{array}{l} \underline{\text{CONTROL}} \text{ IS} \\ \underline{\text{CONTROLS}} \text{ ARE} \end{array} \right\} \left\{ \begin{array}{l} \{\text{data-name-1}\} \ldots \\ \underline{\text{FINAL}} \text{ [data-name-1]} \ldots \end{array} \right\} \right]$$

$$\left[\underline{\text{PAGE}} \left[\begin{array}{l} \text{LIMIT IS} \\ \text{LIMITS ARE} \end{array} \right] \text{integer-1} \left[\begin{array}{l} \text{LINE} \\ \text{LINES} \end{array} \right] \text{[\underline{HEADING} integer-2]} \right.$$

$$\text{[\underline{FIRST} \underline{DETAIL} integer-3]} \quad \text{[\underline{LAST} \underline{DETAIL} integer-4]}$$

$$\left. \text{[\underline{FOOTING} integer-5]} \right] .$$

  General Format for Report Group Description Entry

FORMAT 1

01 [data-name-1]

$$\left[\underline{\text{LINE}} \text{ NUMBER IS} \left\{ \begin{array}{l} \text{integer-1} \quad \text{[ON \underline{NEXT} \underline{PAGE}]} \\ \underline{\text{PLUS}} \text{ integer-2} \end{array} \right\} \right]$$

$$\left[\underline{\text{NEXT}} \underline{\text{GROUP}} \text{ IS} \left\{ \begin{array}{l} \text{integer-3} \\ \underline{\text{PLUS}} \text{ integer-4} \\ \underline{\text{NEXT}} \underline{\text{PAGE}} \end{array} \right\} \right]$$

$$\text{TYPE IS} \left\{ \begin{array}{l} \left\{ \begin{array}{l} \underline{\text{REPORT}}\ \underline{\text{HEADING}} \\ \underline{\text{RH}} \end{array} \right\} \\ \left\{ \begin{array}{l} \underline{\text{PAGE}}\ \underline{\text{HEADING}} \\ \underline{\text{PH}} \end{array} \right\} \\ \left\{ \begin{array}{l} \underline{\text{CONTROL}}\ \underline{\text{HEADING}} \\ \underline{\text{CH}} \end{array} \right\} \left\{ \begin{array}{l} \text{data-name-2} \\ \underline{\text{FINAL}} \end{array} \right\} \\ \left\{ \begin{array}{l} \underline{\text{DETAIL}} \\ \underline{\text{DE}} \end{array} \right\} \\ \left\{ \begin{array}{l} \underline{\text{CONTROL}}\ \underline{\text{FOOTING}} \\ \underline{\text{CF}} \end{array} \right\} \left\{ \begin{array}{l} \text{data-name-3} \\ \underline{\text{FINAL}} \end{array} \right\} \\ \left\{ \begin{array}{l} \underline{\text{PAGE}}\ \underline{\text{FOOTING}} \\ \underline{\text{PF}} \end{array} \right\} \\ \left\{ \begin{array}{l} \underline{\text{REPORT}}\ \underline{\text{FOOTING}} \\ \underline{\text{RF}} \end{array} \right\} \end{array} \right.$$

[[UNDERLINE]]

[[$\underline{\text{USAGE}}$ IS] $\underline{\text{DISPLAY}}$].

FORMAT 2

level-number   [data-name-1]

$$\left[\underline{\text{LINE}}\ \text{NUMBER IS} \left\{ \begin{array}{l} \text{integer-1}\quad [\text{ON}\ \underline{\text{NEXT}}\ \underline{\text{PAGE}}] \\ \underline{\text{PLUS}}\ \text{integer-2} \end{array} \right\} \right]$$

[[$\underline{\text{USAGE}}$ IS] $\underline{\text{DISPLAY}}$].

FORMAT 3

level-number   [data-name-1]

$$\left\{ \begin{matrix} \underline{PICTURE} \\ \underline{PIC} \end{matrix} \right\} \quad IS \quad character\text{-}string$$

[[USAGE IS] DISPLAY]

$$\left[[SIGN IS] \quad \left\{ \begin{matrix} \underline{LEADING} \\ \underline{TRAILING} \end{matrix} \right\} \quad \underline{SEPARATE} \; CHARACTER \right]$$

$$\left[\left\{ \begin{matrix} \underline{JUSTIFIED} \\ \underline{JUST} \end{matrix} \right\} \quad RIGHT \right]$$

[BLANK WHEN ZERO]

$$\left[\underline{LINE} \; NUMBER \; IS \quad \left\{ \begin{matrix} integer\text{-}1 \quad [ON \; \underline{NEXT} \; \underline{PAGE}] \\ \underline{PLUS} \; integer\text{-}2 \end{matrix} \right\} \right]$$

[COLUMN NUMBER IS integer-3]

$$\left\{ \begin{matrix} \underline{SOURCE} \; IS \; identifier\text{-}1 \\ \underline{VALUE} \; IS \; literal\text{-}1 \\ \{\underline{SUM} \; \{identifier\text{-}2\} \; ... \; [\underline{UPON} \; \{data\text{-}name\text{-}2\} \; ... \;] \; \} \; ... \\ \left[\underline{RESET} \; ON \quad \left\{ \begin{matrix} data\text{-}name\text{-}3 \\ \underline{FINAL} \end{matrix} \right\} \right] \end{matrix} \right\}$$

[GROUP INDICATE].

General Format for PROCEDURE DIVISION

FORMAT 1

[PROCEDURE DIVISION [USING {data-name-1} ...] [GIVING identifier-1].
[DECLARATIVES.
{section-name SECTION [segment-number].
   USE statement.
[paragraph-name.
      [sentence] ...] ... } ...
 END DECLARATIVES.]
{section-name SECTION [segment-number].
[paragraph-name.
      [sentence] ...] ... } ...]

FORMAT 2

[PROCEDURE DIVISION [USING {data-name-1} ...] [GIVING identifier-1].
{paragraph-name.
      [sentence] ... } ...]

General Format for COBOL Verbs

ACCEPT identifier-1 [FROM mnemonic-name-1]
      [AT END imperative statement-1]
      [NOT AT END imperative statement-2]
      [END-ACCEPT]

$$\underline{\text{ACCEPT}} \text{ identifier-2 } \underline{\text{FROM}} \left\{ \begin{array}{l} \underline{\text{DATE}} \\ \underline{\text{DAY}} \\ \underline{\text{DAY-OF-WEEK}} \\ \underline{\text{TIME}} \end{array} \right\}$$

$\underline{\text{ACCEPT}}$ dest-item

$$\left\{ \begin{array}{l} \text{FROM } \underline{\text{LINE}} \text{ NUMBER} \left\{ \begin{array}{l} \text{line-num} \\ \text{line-id } [\underline{\text{PLUS}} \text{ [plus-num]]} \\ \underline{\text{PLUS}} \text{ [plus-num]} \end{array} \right\} \\ \\ \text{FROM } \underline{\text{COLUMN}} \text{ NUMBER} \left\{ \begin{array}{l} \text{column-num} \\ \text{column-id } [\underline{\text{PLUS}} \text{ [plus-num]]} \\ \underline{\text{PLUS}} \text{ [plus-num]} \end{array} \right\} \\ \\ \underline{\text{ERASE}} \text{ [TO } \underline{\text{END}} \text{ OF]} \left\{ \begin{array}{l} \underline{\text{SCREEN}} \\ \underline{\text{LINE}} \end{array} \right\} \\ \\ \text{WITH } \underline{\text{BELL}} \\ \underline{\text{UNDERLINED}} \\ \underline{\text{BOLD}} \\ \text{WITH } \underline{\text{BLINKING}} \\ \\ \underline{\text{PROTECTED}} \left[\left\{ \begin{array}{l} \underline{\text{SIZE}} \left\{ \begin{array}{l} \text{prot-size-lit} \\ \text{prot-size-item} \end{array} \right\} \\ \text{WITH } \underline{\text{AUTOTERMINATE}} \\ \text{WITH } \underline{\text{NO BLANK}} \\ \text{WITH } \underline{\text{FILLER}} \text{ prot-fill-lit} \end{array} \right\} \right] \end{array} \right\}$$

```
│ │  WITH CONVERSION                                          │ │
│ │  REVERSED                                                 │ │
│ │  WITH NO ECHO                                             │ │
│ │                        ⎧ def-src-lit   ⎫                  │ │
│ │  DEFAULT IS            ⎨ def-src-item  ⎬                  │ │
│ │                        ⎩ CURRENT VALUE ⎭                  │ │
└ │  CONTROL KEY IN key-dest-item                             │ ┘

   ⎡ ⎧ [ON EXCEPTION stment] [NOT ON EXCEPTION stment2] ⎫ ⎤
   ⎢ ⎨ [AT END stment] [NOT AT END stment2]             ⎬ ⎥
   ⎣ ⎩                                                   ⎭ ⎦

   [END-ACCEPT]
ACCEPT   CONTROL KEY IN key-dest-item

┌ │                        ⎧ line-num                     ⎫   │ ┐
│ │  FROM LINE NUMBER      ⎨ line-id [PLUS  [plus-num]]    ⎬   │ │
│ │                        ⎩ PLUS [plus-num]              ⎭   │ │
│ │                                                           │ │
│ │                        ⎧ column-num                   ⎫   │ │
⎨ │  FROM COLUMN NUMBER    ⎨ column-id [PLUS  [plus-num]]  ⎬   │ ⎬
│ │                        ⎩ PLUS [plus-num]              ⎭   │ │
│ │                                                           │ │
│ │                                  ⎧ SCREEN ⎫               │ │
│ │  ERASE  [TO END OF]              ⎨ LINE   ⎬               │ │
└ │  WITH BELL                       ⎩        ⎭               │ ┘

   ⎡ ⎧ [ON EXCEPTION stment] [NOT ON EXCEPTION stment2] ⎫ ⎤
   ⎢ ⎨ [AT END stment] [NOT AT END stment2]             ⎬ ⎥
   ⎣ ⎩                                                   ⎭ ⎦
```

[END-ACCEPT]

ACCEPT cd-name-1 MESSAGE COUNT

ADD $\begin{Bmatrix} \text{identifier-1} \\ \text{literal-1} \end{Bmatrix}$ ... TO {identifier-2 [ROUNDED]} ...

   [ON SIZE ERROR imperative-statement-1]
   [NOT ON SIZE ERROR imperative-statement-2]
   [END-ADD]

ADD $\begin{Bmatrix} \text{identifier-1} \\ \text{literal-1} \end{Bmatrix}$ ... TO $\begin{Bmatrix} \text{identifier-2} \\ \text{literal-2} \end{Bmatrix}$

   GIVING {identifier-3 [ROUNDED]} ...
   [ON SIZE ERROR imperative-statement-1]
   [NOT ON SIZE ERROR imperative-statement-2]
   [END-ADD]

ADD $\begin{Bmatrix} \text{CORRESPONDING} \\ \text{CORR} \end{Bmatrix}$ identifier-1 TO identifier-2 [ROUNDED]

   [ON SIZE ERROR imperative-statement-1]
   [NOT ON SIZE ERROR imperative-statement-2]
   [END-ADD]

ALTER {procedure-name-1 TO [PROCEED TO] procedure-name-2} ...

CALL $\begin{Bmatrix} \text{identifier-1} \\ \text{literal-1} \end{Bmatrix}$ $\left[\text{USING} \begin{Bmatrix} \text{[BY REFERENCE] \{identifier-2\} ...} \\ \text{BY CONTENT \{identifier-2\} ...} \end{Bmatrix} ... \right]$

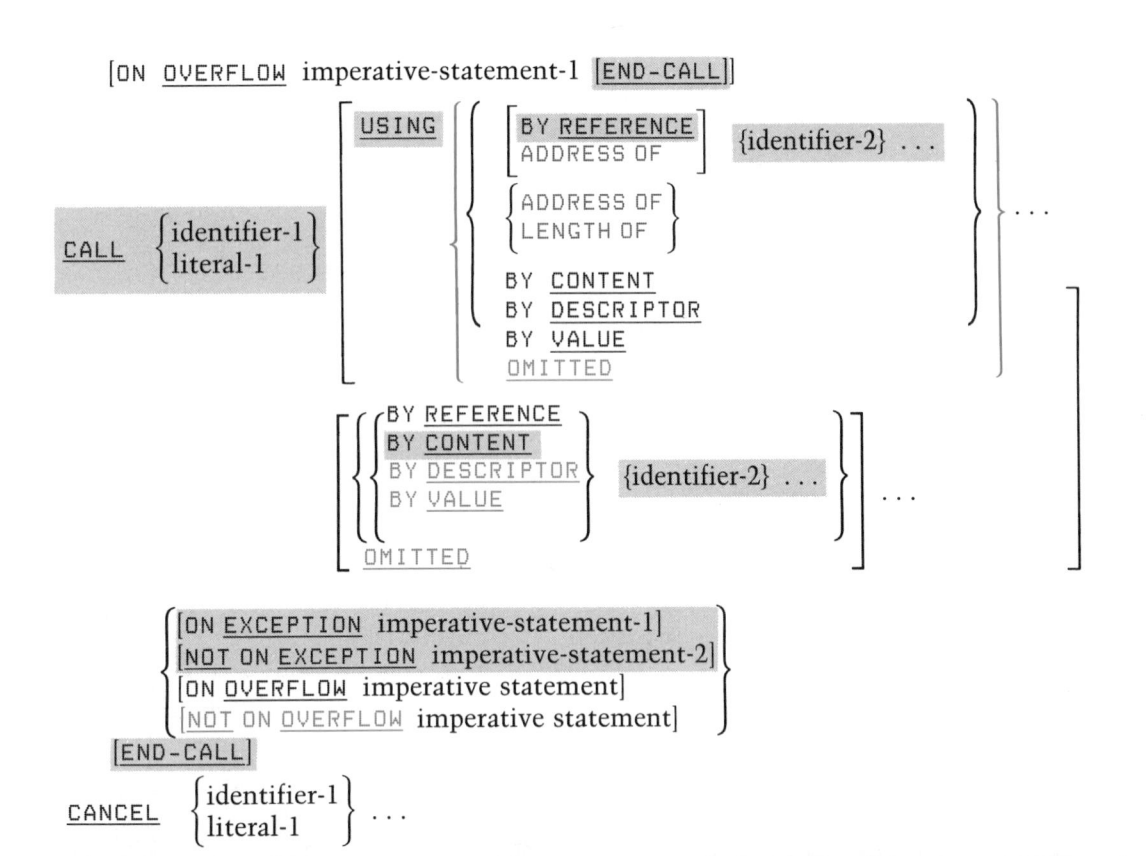

```
                    [ON OVERFLOW imperative-statement-1 [END-CALL]]

                              ⎡        ⎧ ⎡BY REFERENCE⎤                      ⎫   ⎤
                              ⎢ USING  ⎪ ⎣ADDRESS OF  ⎦ {identifier-2} ...   ⎪   ⎥
                              ⎢        ⎪                                     ⎪   ⎥
                              ⎢        ⎪ ⎧ADDRESS OF⎫                        ⎪   ⎥
CALL  ⎧identifier-1⎫          ⎢        ⎨ ⎩LENGTH OF ⎭                        ⎬ ...
      ⎩literal-1   ⎭          ⎢        ⎪                                     ⎪
                              ⎢        ⎪ BY CONTENT                          ⎪
                              ⎢        ⎪ BY DESCRIPTOR                       ⎪
                              ⎢        ⎪ BY VALUE                            ⎪
                              ⎢        ⎩ OMITTED                             ⎭

                              ⎢   ⎡ ⎧BY REFERENCE  ⎫                     ⎫
                              ⎢   ⎢ ⎪BY CONTENT    ⎪                     ⎪
                              ⎢   ⎢ ⎨BY DESCRIPTOR ⎬ {identifier-2} ... ⎬ ...
                              ⎢   ⎢ ⎩BY VALUE      ⎭                     ⎪
                              ⎣   ⎣ OMITTED                             ⎭

                        ⎧ [ON EXCEPTION imperative-statement-1]       ⎫
                        ⎪ [NOT ON EXCEPTION imperative-statement-2]   ⎪
                        ⎨ [ON OVERFLOW imperative statement]          ⎬
                        ⎩ [NOT ON OVERFLOW imperative statement]      ⎭

                   [END-CALL]

CANCEL  ⎧identifier-1⎫ ...
        ⎩literal-1   ⎭
```

SW CLOSE $\left\{ \text{file-name-1} \left[\begin{array}{l} \left\{ \begin{array}{l} \underline{REEL} \\ \underline{UNIT} \end{array} \right\} \quad [\text{FOR } \underline{REMOVAL}] \\ \text{WITH} \quad \left\{ \begin{array}{l} \underline{NO} \underline{REWIND} \\ \underline{LOCK} \end{array} \right\} \end{array} \right] \right\}$ ...

RI CLOSE {file-name-1 [WITH LOCK]} ...

COMMIT [RETAINING]
    [ON ERROR stment]
    [NOT ON ERROR stment2]
    [END-COMMIT]

COMPUTE {identifier-1 [ROUNDED]} ... $\left\{ \begin{array}{l} = \\ \text{EQUAL} \end{array} \right\}$ arithmetic-expression-1

    [ON SIZE ERROR imperative-statement-1]
    [NOT ON SIZE ERROR imperative-statement-2]
    [END-COMPUTE]

CONNECT [record-name] TO $\left\{ \begin{array}{l} \{\text{set-name}\} \dots \\ \underline{ALL} \end{array} \right\}$

$\left[\text{RETAINING} \left\{ \left(\left| \begin{array}{l} \underline{REALM} \\ \underline{RECORD} \\ \left\{ \begin{array}{l} \underline{SET} \text{ [set-name]} \dots \\ \{\text{set-name}\} \dots \end{array} \right\} \end{array} \right| \right) \right\} \text{CURRENCY} \right]$

[ON ERROR stment] [NOT ON ERROR stment2]
[END-CONNECT]

40

CONTINUE
DELETE file-name-1 RECORD
    [INVALID KEY imperative-statement-1]
    [NOT INVALID KEY imperative-statement-2]
    [END-DELETE]

DISABLE $\left\{\begin{array}{l} \text{INPUT [TERMINAL]} \\ \text{I-O TERMINAL} \\ \text{OUTPUT} \end{array}\right\}$ cd-name-1

DISCONNECT [record-name] FROM $\left\{\begin{array}{l} \text{\{set-name\} ...} \\ \text{ALL} \end{array}\right\}$

    [ON ERROR stment]
    [NOT ON ERROR stment2]
    [END-DISCONNECT]

DISPLAY $\left\{\begin{array}{l} \text{identifier-1} \\ \text{literal-1} \end{array}\right\}$ ... [UPON $\left\{\begin{array}{l} \text{CONSOLE} \\ \text{SYSOUT} \\ \text{mnemonic-name-1]} \end{array}\right\}$ [WITH NO ADVANCING]

```
DISPLAY {src-item
              ┌ ┌    ┌ AT LINE NUMBER
              │ │    │
              │ │    │       ⎧ line-num                    ⎫
              │ │    │       ⎨ line-id  [PLUS  [plus-num]] ⎬
              │ │    │       ⎩ PLUS  [plus-num]            ⎭
              │ │    │
              │ │    │   AT COLUMN NUMBER
              │ │    │
              │ │    │       ⎧ column-num                    ⎫
              │ │    ⎨       ⎨ column-id  [PLUS  [plus-num]] ⎬       ⎬  } ...
              │ │    │       ⎩ PLUS  [plus-num]              ⎭
              │ │    │
              │ │    │   ERASE  [TO END OF]  ⎧ SCREEN ⎫
              │ │    │                       ⎩ LINE   ⎭
              │ │    │
              │ │    │   WITH BELL
              │ │    │   UNDERLINED
              │ │    │   BOLD
              │ │    │   WITH BLINKING
              │ │    │   REVERSED
              └ └    │   WITH CONVERSION

                 [WITH NO ADVANCING]

DIVIDE  ⎧ identifier-1 ⎫   INTO  ⎧ identifier-2 ⎫  GIVING identifier-3 [ROUNDED]
        ⎩ literal-1    ⎭         ⎩ literal-2    ⎭

        REMAINDER  identifier-4
        [ON SIZE ERROR  imperative-statement-1]
```

42

[NOT ON SIZE ERROR imperative-statement-2]
[END-DIVIDE]

DIVIDE $\begin{Bmatrix} \text{identifier-1} \\ \text{literal-1} \end{Bmatrix}$ BY $\begin{Bmatrix} \text{identifier-2} \\ \text{literal-2} \end{Bmatrix}$ GIVING identifier-3 [ROUNDED]

REMAINDER identifier-4
[ON SIZE ERROR imperative-statement-1]
[NOT ON SIZE ERROR imperative-statement-2]
[END-DIVIDE]

DIVIDE $\begin{Bmatrix} \text{identifier-1} \\ \text{literal-1} \end{Bmatrix}$ INTO {identifier-2 [ROUNDED]} ...

[ON SIZE ERROR imperative-statement-1]
[NOT ON SIZE ERROR imperative-statement-2]
[END-DIVIDE]

DIVIDE $\begin{Bmatrix} \text{identifier-1} \\ \text{literal-1} \end{Bmatrix}$ INTO $\begin{Bmatrix} \text{identifier-2} \\ \text{literal-2} \end{Bmatrix}$

GIVING {identifier-3 [ROUNDED]} ...
[ON SIZE ERROR imperative-statement-1]
[NOT ON SIZE ERROR imperative-statement-2]
[END-DIVIDE]

DIVIDE $\begin{Bmatrix} \text{identifier-1} \\ \text{literal-1} \end{Bmatrix}$ BY $\begin{Bmatrix} \text{identifier-2} \\ \text{literal-2} \end{Bmatrix}$

GIVING {identifier-3 [ROUNDED]} ...
[ON SIZE ERROR imperative-statement-1]

[<u>NOT</u> ON <u>SIZE</u> <u>ERROR</u> imperative-statement-2]
[<u>END-DIVIDE</u>]

<u>ENABLE</u> { <u>INPUT</u> [<u>TERMINAL</u>]
            <u>I-O</u> <u>TERMINAL</u>
            <u>OUTPUT</u> } cd-name-1

<u>ENTRY</u> literal <u>USING</u> identifier-1 ...

<u>ERASE</u> [<u>ALL</u>] [record-name]
      [ON <u>ERROR</u> stment]
      [<u>NOT</u> ON <u>ERROR</u> stment2]
      [<u>END-ERASE</u>]

<u>EVALUATE</u> { identifier-1
             literal-1
             expression-1
             <u>TRUE</u>
             <u>FALSE</u> } [<u>ALSO</u> { identifier-2
                                      literal-2
                                      expression-2
                                      <u>TRUE</u>
                                      <u>FALSE</u> }] ...

{{<u>WHEN</u>

{ <u>ANY</u>
  condition-1
  <u>TRUE</u>
  <u>FALSE</u>
  [<u>NOT</u>] { identifier-3
             literal-3
             arithmetic-expression-1 } [{ <u>THROUGH</u>
                                           <u>THRU</u> } { identifier-4
                                                        literal-4
                                                        arithmetic-expression-2 }] }}

44

```
[ALSO

  ⎧ ANY                                                                      ⎫
  ⎪ condition-2                                                              ⎪
  ⎨ TRUE                                                                     ⎬
  ⎪ FALSE                                                                    ⎪   ⎤⎤      ⎫
  ⎪        ⎧ identifier-5          ⎫ ⎡ ⎧ THROUGH ⎫ ⎧ identifier-6          ⎫ ⎤⎪   ⎪⎪ ...  ⎬ ...
  ⎩ [NOT]  ⎨ literal-5             ⎬ ⎢ ⎨ THRU    ⎬ ⎨ literal-6             ⎬ ⎥⎭   ⎦⎦      ⎭
           ⎩ arithmetic-expression-3 ⎭ ⎣ ⎩        ⎭ ⎩ arithmetic-expression-4 ⎭ ⎦

  imperative-statement-1} ...
  [WHEN OTHER imperative-statement-2]
  [END-EVALUATE]
  EXIT
  EXIT PROGRAM
FETCH database-record
     [FOR UPDATE]

  ⎡                ⎡⎧⎪ REALM             ⎫⎤          ⎤
  ⎢                ⎢⎪  RECORD            ⎪⎥          ⎥
  ⎢ RETAINING      ⎢⎨                    ⎬⎥ CURRENCY ⎥
  ⎢                ⎢⎪  SET [set-name] ...⎪⎥          ⎥
  ⎣                ⎣⎩  {set-name} ...    ⎭⎦          ⎦

  ⎡⎧ [AT END stment] [NOT AT END stment2]    ⎫⎤
  ⎣⎩ [ON ERROR stment] [NOT ON ERROR stment2]⎭⎦
  [END-FETCH]
```

```
FIND database-record [FOR UPDATE]
      ┌                ┌┌│  REALM                  ││┐            ┐
      │ RETAINING      │││  RECORD                 │││ CURRENCY   │
      │                │││ ┌SET [set-name] ...┐    │││            │
      │                │││ {set-name} ...     }    ││┘            │
      └                └└│ └                  ┘    │┘            ┘
      ┌ ┌ [AT END stment] [NOT AT END stment2]   ┐ ┐
      │ { [ON ERROR stment] [NOT ON ERROR stment2] } │
      └ └                                         ┘ ┘
      [END-FIND]

FIND ALL keeplist-name [record-name]  ┌ WITHIN {realm-name} ┐
                                       └        {set-name  } ┘
      ┌ USING {rec-key} ...   ┐
      │ WHERE {bool-expres}   │  [FOR UPDATE]
      └                       ┘
      ┌ ┌ [AT END stment] [NOT AT END stment2]   ┐ ┐
      │ { [ON ERROR stment] [NOT ON ERROR stment2] } │
      └ └                                         ┘ ┘
      [END-FIND]

FREE  ┌ database-key-id                              ┐
      │      ┌ ┌ FROM {keeplist-name} ... ┐ ┐        │
      │ ALL  │ │ CURRENT                  │ │        │
      └      └ └                          ┘ ┘        ┘
      [ON ERROR stment]
      [NOT ON ERROR stment2]
      [END-FREE]
```

46

GENERATE $\left\{\begin{array}{l}\text{data-name-1}\\\text{report-name-1}\end{array}\right\}$

GET $\left[\begin{array}{l}\text{record-name}\\\{\text{record-item}\}\ldots\end{array}\right]$

[ON ERROR stment]

[NOT ON ERROR stment2]

[END-GET]

[GOBACK]

GO TO [procedure-name-1]
GO TO {procedure-name-1}... DEPENDING ON identifier-1

IF condition-1 THEN $\left\{\begin{array}{l}\{\text{statement-1}\}\ldots\\\text{NEXT SENTENCE}\end{array}\right\}$ $\left\{\begin{array}{l}\underline{\text{ELSE}}\ \{\text{statement-2}\}\ldots\ \boxed{\text{END-IF}}\\\underline{\text{ELSE NEXT SENTENCE}}\\\underline{\text{END-IF}}\end{array}\right\}$

INITIALIZE {identifier-1}...

$\left[\begin{array}{l}\text{REPLACING}\ \left\{\begin{array}{l}\left\{\begin{array}{l}\text{ALPHABETIC}\\\text{ALPHANUMERIC}\\\text{NUMERIC}\\\text{ALPHANUMERIC-EDITED}\\\text{NUMERIC-EDITED}\\\text{BBCS}\\\text{EGCS}\end{array}\right\}\ \text{DATA}\ \underline{\text{BY}}\ \left\{\begin{array}{l}\text{identifier-2}\\\text{literal-1}\end{array}\right\}\end{array}\right\}\ldots\end{array}\right]$

```
INITIATE  {report-name-1} ...
INSPECT identifier-1 TALLYING

    ⎧                   ⎧ CHARACTERS ⎡ ⎧BEFORE⎫ INITIAL ⎧identifier-4⎫ ⎤ ...              ⎫     ⎫
    ⎪                   ⎪            ⎣ ⎨AFTER ⎬         ⎨literal-2   ⎬ ⎦                  ⎪     ⎪
    ⎪ identifier-2 FOR  ⎨            ⎩      ⎭                                             ⎬ ... ⎬ ...
    ⎪                   ⎪ ⎧ALL    ⎫ ⎧identifier-3⎫ ⎡ ⎧BEFORE⎫ INITIAL ⎧identifier-4⎫ ⎤ ... ⎪     ⎪
    ⎩                   ⎩ ⎨LEADING⎬ ⎨literal-1   ⎬ ⎣ ⎨AFTER ⎬         ⎨literal-2   ⎬ ⎦      ⎭     ⎭
                          ⎩       ⎭ ⎩            ⎭   ⎩      ⎭

INSPECT identifier-1 REPLACING

    ⎧ CHARACTERS BY ⎧identifier-5⎫ ⎡ ⎧BEFORE⎫ INITIAL ⎧identifier-4⎫ ⎤ ...                             ⎫
    ⎪               ⎨literal-3   ⎬ ⎣ ⎨AFTER ⎬         ⎨literal-2   ⎬ ⎦                                 ⎪
    ⎪               ⎩            ⎭   ⎩      ⎭                                                          ⎪ ...
    ⎪ ⎧ALL    ⎫ ⎧identifier-3⎫ BY ⎧identifier-5⎫ ⎡ ⎧BEFORE⎫ INITIAL ⎧identifier-4⎫ ⎤ ...              ⎪
    ⎨ ⎨LEADING⎬ ⎨literal-1   ⎬    ⎨literal-3   ⎬ ⎣ ⎨AFTER ⎬         ⎨literal-2   ⎬ ⎦                  ⎬
    ⎩ ⎩FIRST  ⎭ ⎩            ⎭    ⎩            ⎭   ⎩      ⎭                                            ⎭

INSPECT identifier-1 TALLYING

    ⎧                   ⎧ CHARACTERS ⎡ ⎧BEFORE⎫ INITIAL ⎧identifier-4⎫ ⎤ ...              ⎫     ⎫
    ⎪                   ⎪            ⎣ ⎨AFTER ⎬         ⎨literal-2   ⎬ ⎦                  ⎪     ⎪
    ⎪ identifier-2 FOR  ⎨            ⎩      ⎭                                             ⎬ ... ⎬ ...
    ⎪                   ⎪ ⎧ALL    ⎫ ⎧identifier-3⎫ ⎡ ⎧BEFORE⎫ INITIAL ⎧identifier-4⎫ ⎤ ... ⎪     ⎪
    ⎩                   ⎩ ⎨LEADING⎬ ⎨literal-1   ⎬ ⎣ ⎨AFTER ⎬         ⎨literal-2   ⎬ ⎦      ⎭     ⎭
                          ⎩       ⎭ ⎩            ⎭   ⎩      ⎭
```

48

REPLACING

$$\left\{ \begin{array}{l} \underline{\text{CHARACTERS}} \ \underline{\text{BY}} \ \left\{ \begin{array}{l} \text{identifier-5} \\ \text{literal-3} \end{array} \right\} \ \left[\left\{ \begin{array}{l} \underline{\text{BEFORE}} \\ \underline{\text{AFTER}} \end{array} \right\} \ \text{INITIAL} \ \left\{ \begin{array}{l} \text{identifier-4} \\ \text{literal-2} \end{array} \right\} \right] \ \dots \\ \left\{ \begin{array}{l} \underline{\text{ALL}} \\ \underline{\text{LEADING}} \\ \underline{\text{FIRST}} \end{array} \right\} \left\{ \left\{ \begin{array}{l} \text{identifier-3} \\ \text{literal-1} \end{array} \right\} \ \underline{\text{BY}} \ \left\{ \begin{array}{l} \text{identifier-5} \\ \text{literal-3} \end{array} \right\} \ \left[\left\{ \begin{array}{l} \underline{\text{BEFORE}} \\ \underline{\text{AFTER}} \end{array} \right\} \ \text{INITIAL} \ \left\{ \begin{array}{l} \text{identifier-4} \\ \text{literal-2} \end{array} \right\} \right] \dots \right\} \dots \end{array} \right\} \dots$$

$$\underline{\text{INSPECT}} \ \text{identifier-1} \ \underline{\text{CONVERTING}} \ \left\{ \begin{array}{l} \text{identifier-6} \\ \text{literal-4} \end{array} \right\} \ \underline{\text{TO}} \ \left\{ \begin{array}{l} \text{identifier-7} \\ \text{literal-5} \end{array} \right\}$$

$$\left[\left\{ \begin{array}{l} \underline{\text{BEFORE}} \\ \underline{\text{AFTER}} \end{array} \right\} \ \text{INITIAL} \ \left\{ \begin{array}{l} \text{identifier-4} \\ \text{literal-2} \end{array} \right\} \right] \dots$$

$\underline{\text{KEEP}}$ [database-key-id] $\underline{\text{USING}}$ destination-keeplist

    [ON $\underline{\text{ERROR}}$ imperative statement-1]
    [$\underline{\text{NOT}}$ ON $\underline{\text{ERROR}}$ imperative statement-2]
    [END-KEEP]

$$\underline{\text{MERGE}} \ \text{file-name-1} \ \left\{ \text{ON} \ \left\{ \begin{array}{l} \underline{\text{ASCENDING}} \\ \underline{\text{DESCENDING}} \end{array} \right\} \ \text{KEY} \ \{\text{data-name-1}\} \dots \right\} \dots$$

    [COLLATING $\underline{\text{SEQUENCE}}$ IS alphabet-name-1]
$\underline{\text{USING}}$ file-name-2   {file-name-3} . . .

$$\left\{ \begin{array}{l} \underline{\text{OUTPUT PROCEDURE}} \ \text{IS procedure-name-1} \ \left[\left\{ \begin{array}{l} \underline{\text{THROUGH}} \\ \underline{\text{THRU}} \end{array} \right\} \ \text{procedure-name-2} \right] \\ \underline{\text{GIVING}} \ \ \{\text{file-name-4}\} \dots \end{array} \right\}$$

MODIFY $\begin{bmatrix} \text{record-name} \\ \{\text{record-item}\}\ \ldots \end{bmatrix}$

$\left[\underline{\text{RETAINING}} \left[\left\{ \begin{array}{l} \left| \begin{array}{l} \underline{\text{REALM}} \\ \underline{\text{RECORD}} \\ \underline{\text{SET}}\ [\text{set-name}]\ \ldots \\ \{\text{set-name}\}\ \ldots \end{array} \right| \end{array} \right\} \right] \text{CURRENCY} \right]$

[ON ERROR stment]
[NOT ON ERROR stment2]
[END-MODIFY]

MOVE $\left\{ \begin{array}{l} \text{identifier-1} \\ \text{literal-1} \end{array} \right\}$ TO {identifier-2} ...

MOVE $\left\{ \begin{array}{l} \underline{\text{CORRESPONDING}} \\ \underline{\text{CORR}} \end{array} \right\}$ identifier-1 TO identifier-2

MULTIPLY $\left\{ \begin{array}{l} \text{identifier-1} \\ \text{literal-1} \end{array} \right\}$ BY {identifier-2 [ROUNDED]} ...

[ON SIZE ERROR imperative-statement-1]
[NOT ON SIZE ERROR imperative-statement-2]
[END-MULTIPLY]

MULTIPLY $\left\{ \begin{array}{l} \text{identifier-1} \\ \text{literal-1} \end{array} \right\}$ BY $\left\{ \begin{array}{l} \text{identifier-2} \\ \text{literal-2} \end{array} \right\}$

50

GIVING {identifier-3 [ROUNDED]} . . .
[ON SIZE ERROR imperative-statement-1]
[NOT ON SIZE ERROR imperative-statement-2]
[END-MULTIPLY]

S OPEN

$$\left\{\begin{array}{l} \text{INPUT \{file-name-1 [WITH NO REWIND]\} . . .} \\ \text{OUTPUT \{file-name-2 [WITH NO REWIND]\} . . .} \\ \left[\text{ALLOWING} \left[\left\{\begin{array}{l}\text{NO OTHERS}\\ \left\{\begin{array}{l}\text{READERS}\\ \text{WRITERS}\\ \text{UPDATERS}\\ \text{ALL}\end{array}\right\}\end{array}\right\}\right]\right] \end{array}\right\} . . .$$

I-O {file-name-3} . . .
EXTEND {file-name-4} . . .

RI OPEN

$$\left\{\begin{array}{l} \text{INPUT \{file-name-1\} . . .} \\ \text{OUTPUT \{file-name-2\} . . .} \\ \left[\text{ALLOWING} \left[\left\{\begin{array}{l}\text{NO OTHERS}\\ \left\{\begin{array}{l}\text{READERS}\\ \text{WRITERS}\\ \text{UPDATERS}\\ \text{ALL}\end{array}\right\}\end{array}\right\}\right]\right] \end{array}\right\} . . .$$

I-O {file-name-3} . . .
EXTEND {file-name-4} . . .

W OPEN $\left\{ \begin{array}{l} \underline{OUTPUT} \text{ \{file-name-1 [WITH \underline{NO} \underline{REWIND}]\}} \dots \\ \underline{EXTEND} \text{ \{file-name-2\}} \dots \end{array} \right\} \dots$

$\underline{PERFORM} \left[\text{procedure-name-1} \left[\left\{ \begin{array}{l} \underline{THROUGH} \\ \underline{THRU} \end{array} \right\} \text{procedure-name-2} \right] \right]$

[imperative-statement-1 END-PERFORM]

$\underline{PERFORM} \left[\text{procedure-name-1} \left[\left\{ \begin{array}{l} \underline{THROUGH} \\ \underline{THRU} \end{array} \right\} \text{procedure-name-2} \right] \right]$

$\left\{ \begin{array}{l} \text{identifier-1} \\ \text{integer-1} \end{array} \right\}$ $\underline{TIMES}$ [imperative-statement-1 END-PERFORM]

$\underline{PERFORM} \left[\text{procedure-name-1} \left[\left\{ \begin{array}{l} \underline{THROUGH} \\ \underline{THRU} \end{array} \right\} \text{procedure-name-2} \right] \right]$

$\left[\text{WITH } \underline{TEST} \left\{ \begin{array}{l} \underline{BEFORE} \\ \underline{AFTER} \end{array} \right\} \right] \underline{UNTIL} \text{ condition-1}$

[imperative-statement-1 END-PERFORM]

$\underline{PERFORM} \left[\text{procedure-name-1} \left[\left\{ \begin{array}{l} \underline{THROUGH} \\ \underline{THRU} \end{array} \right\} \text{procedure-name-2} \right] \right]$

$\left[\text{WITH } \underline{TEST} \left\{ \begin{array}{l} \underline{BEFORE} \\ \underline{AFTER} \end{array} \right\} \right]$

$\underline{VARYING} \left\{ \begin{array}{l} \text{identifier-2} \\ \text{index-name-1} \end{array} \right\} \underline{FROM} \left\{ \begin{array}{l} \text{identifier-3} \\ \text{index-name-2} \\ \text{literal-1} \end{array} \right\}$

$$\underline{BY} \left\{ \begin{array}{l} \text{identifier-4} \\ \text{literal-2} \end{array} \right\} \quad \underline{UNTIL} \text{ condition-1}$$

$$\left[\underline{AFTER} \left\{ \begin{array}{l} \text{identifier-5} \\ \text{index-name-3} \end{array} \right\} \quad \underline{FROM} \left\{ \begin{array}{l} \text{identifier-6} \\ \text{index-name-4} \\ \text{literal-3} \end{array} \right\} \right.$$

$$\left. \underline{BY} \left\{ \begin{array}{l} \text{identifier-7} \\ \text{literal-4} \end{array} \right\} \quad \underline{UNTIL} \text{ condition-2} \right] \dots$$

[imperative-statement-1 `END-PERFORM`]

```
       PURGE cd-name-1
 SRI  READ file-name-1  [NEXT]  RECORD  [INTO identifier-1]
```

$$\left[\begin{array}{l} \text{REGARDLESS OF LOCK} \\ \\ \text{ALLOWING} \left\{ \begin{array}{l} \text{UPDATERS} \\ \text{READERS} \\ \text{NO OTHERS} \end{array} \right\} \end{array} \right]$$

[AT `END` imperative-statement-1]
[`NOT` AT `END` imperative-statement-2]
[`END-READ`]
R `READ` file-name-1 `RECORD` [`INTO` identifier-1]

```
      ┌ REGARDLESS OF LOCK                  ┐
      │                                     │
      │             ┌ UPDATERS  ┐           │
      │ ALLOWING    │ READERS   │           │
      │             └ NO OTHERS ┘           │
      └                                     ┘

      [INVALID KEY imperative-statement-3]
      [NOT INVALID KEY imperative-statement-4]
      [END-READ]
I READ file-name-1 RECORD   [INTO identifier-1]
      [KEY IS data-name-1]
      [INVALID KEY imperative-statement-3]
      [NOT INVALID KEY imperative-statement-4]
      [END-READ]
READY [realm-name] ...
           ┌                                                              ┐
           │              ┌ CONCURRENT ┐ ┌ ┌ RETRIEVAL ┐ ┐               │
           │              │ EXCLUSIVE  │ │ │ UPDATE    │ │               │
           │              │ PROTECTED  │ └ └           ┘ ┘               │
           │              └ BATCH      ┘                                 │
           │ USAGE-MODE IS                                               │
           │                            ┌ CONCURRENT ┐                   │
           │              ┌ RETRIEVAL ┐ │ EXCLUSIVE  │                   │
           │              │ UPDATE    │ │ PROTECTED  │                   │
           │              └           ┘ └ BATCH      ┘                   │
           └                                                              ┘
    [WITH WAIT]
    [ON ERROR imperative statement-1]
    [NOT ON ERROR imperative statement-2]
    [END-READY]
```

RECEIVE cd-name-1 $\begin{Bmatrix} \underline{\text{MESSAGE}} \\ \underline{\text{SEGMENT}} \end{Bmatrix}$ INTO identifier-1

    [NO DATA imperative-statement-1]
    [WITH DATA imperative-statement-2]
    [END-RECEIVE]

RECONNECT [record-name] WITHIN $\begin{Bmatrix} \{\text{set-name}\} \dots \\ \underline{\text{ALL}} \end{Bmatrix}$

$$\left[\text{RETAINING} \left[\left\{ \left| \begin{array}{l} \underline{\text{REALM}} \\ \underline{\text{RECORD}} \\ \begin{Bmatrix} \underline{\text{SET}} \text{ [set-name]} \dots \\ \{\text{set-name}\} \dots \end{Bmatrix} \end{array} \right| \right\} \right] \text{CURRENCY} \right]$$

    [ON ERROR stment]
    [NOT ON ERROR stment2]
    [END-RECONNECT]
RELEASE record-name-1 [FROM identifier-1]
RETURN file-name-1 RECORD [INTO identifier-1]
    AT END imperative-statement-1
    [NOT AT END imperative-statement-2]
    [END-RETURN]
S REWRITE record-name-1 [FROM identifier-1]
RI REWRITE record-name-1 [FROM identifier-1]
    [ALLOWING NO OTHERS]
    [INVALID KEY imperative-statement-1]

[NOT INVALID KEY imperative-statement-2]
[END-REWRITE]
ROLLBACK
   [ON ERROR stment]
   [NOT ON ERROR stment2]
   [END-ROLLBACK]

SEARCH identifier-1 $\left[\underline{\text{VARYING}} \begin{Bmatrix} \text{identifier-2} \\ \text{index-name-1} \end{Bmatrix} \right]$

   [AT END imperative-statement-1]

   $\left\{ \underline{\text{WHEN}} \text{ condition-1} \begin{Bmatrix} \text{imperative-statement-2} \\ \underline{\text{NEXT}}\ \underline{\text{SENTENCE}} \end{Bmatrix} \right\} \ldots$

   [END-SEARCH]

SEARCH ALL identifier-1   [AT END imperative-statement-1]

$\underline{\text{WHEN}} \left\{ \begin{matrix} \text{data-name-1} \begin{Bmatrix} \text{IS } \underline{\text{EQUAL}} \text{ TO} \\ \text{IS =} \end{Bmatrix} \begin{Bmatrix} \text{identifier-3} \\ \text{literal-1} \\ \text{arithmetic-expression-1} \end{Bmatrix} \\ \text{condition-name-1} \end{matrix} \right\}$

$\left[\underline{\text{AND}} \left\{ \begin{matrix} \text{data-name-2} \begin{Bmatrix} \text{IS } \underline{\text{EQUAL}} \text{ TO} \\ \text{IS =} \end{Bmatrix} \begin{Bmatrix} \text{identifier-4} \\ \text{literal-2} \\ \text{arithmetic-expression-2} \end{Bmatrix} \\ \text{condition-name-2} \end{matrix} \right\} \right] \ldots$

56

$$\left\{\begin{array}{l}\text{imperative-statement-2}\\\underline{\text{NEXT}}\ \underline{\text{SENTENCE}}\end{array}\right\}$$

[END-SEARCH]

$\underline{\text{SEND}}$ cd-name-1 $\underline{\text{FROM}}$ identifier-1

$\underline{\text{SEND}}$ cd-name-1 $\quad$ [$\underline{\text{FROM}}$ identifier-1] $\left\{\begin{array}{l}\text{WITH identifier-2}\\\text{WITH }\underline{\text{ESI}}\\\text{WITH }\underline{\text{EMI}}\\\text{WITH }\underline{\text{EGI}}\end{array}\right\}$

$$\left[\left\{\begin{array}{l}\underline{\text{BEFORE}}\\\underline{\text{AFTER}}\end{array}\right\}\ \text{ADVANCING}\ \left\{\begin{array}{l}\left\{\begin{array}{l}\text{identifier-3}\\\text{integer-1}\end{array}\right\}\left[\begin{array}{l}\text{LINE}\\\text{LINES}\end{array}\right]\\\left\{\begin{array}{l}\text{mnemonic-name-1}\\\underline{\text{PAGE}}\end{array}\right\}\end{array}\right\}\right]$$

[REPLACING LINE]

$\underline{\text{SET}}\quad\left\{\begin{array}{l}\text{index-name-1}\\\text{identifier-1}\end{array}\right\}\ \dots\ \underline{\text{TO}}\left\{\begin{array}{l}\text{index-name-2}\\\text{identifier-2}\\\text{integer-1}\end{array}\right\}$

$\underline{\text{SET}}\quad\{\text{index-name-3}\}\ \dots\ \left\{\begin{array}{l}\underline{\text{UP}}\ \underline{\text{BY}}\\\underline{\text{DOWN}}\ \underline{\text{BY}}\end{array}\right\}\ \left\{\begin{array}{l}\text{identifier-3}\\\text{integer-2}\end{array}\right\}$

$\underline{\text{SET}}\quad\left\{\{\text{mnemonic-name-1}\}\ \dots\ \underline{\text{TO}}\left\{\begin{array}{l}\underline{\text{ON}}\\\underline{\text{OFF}}\end{array}\right\}\right\}\ \dots$

<u>SET</u> {condition-name-1} ... <u>TO TRUE</u>

<u>SET</u> pointer-id <u>TO REFERENCE</u> OF identifier

<u>SET</u> status-code-id <u>TO</u> $\left\{ \begin{array}{l} \underline{SUCCESS} \\ \underline{FAILURE} \end{array} \right\}$

<u>SET</u> $\left\{ \begin{array}{l} \text{identifier} \\ \underline{ADDRESS} \text{ OF identifier} \end{array} \right\}$ <u>TO</u> $\left\{ \begin{array}{l} \text{identifier} \\ \underline{ADDRESS} \text{ OF identifier} \\ \underline{NULL} \\ \underline{NULLS} \end{array} \right\}$

<u>SORT</u> file-name-1 $\left\{ \text{ON} \left\{ \begin{array}{l} \underline{ASCENDING} \\ \underline{DESCENDING} \end{array} \right\} \text{KEY} \{\text{data-name-1}\} \dots \right\} \dots$

[WITH <u>DUPLICATES</u> IN ORDER]

[<u>COLLATING</u> <u>SEQUENCE</u> IS alphabet-name-1]

$\left\{ \begin{array}{l} \underline{INPUT} \; \underline{PROCEDURE} \; \text{IS procedure-name-1} \quad \left[\left\{ \begin{array}{l} \underline{THROUGH} \\ \underline{THRU} \end{array} \right\} \text{procedure-name-2} \right] \\ \\ \underline{USING} \; \{\text{file-name-2}\} \dots \end{array} \right\}$

$\left\{ \begin{array}{l} \underline{OUTPUT} \; \underline{PROCEDURE} \; \text{IS procedure-name-3} \quad \left[\left\{ \begin{array}{l} \underline{THROUGH} \\ \underline{THRU} \end{array} \right\} \text{procedure-name-4} \right] \\ \\ \underline{GIVING} \; \{\text{file-name-3}\} \dots \end{array} \right\}$

58

```
                         ┌ IS EQUAL TO          ┐
                         │ IS =                 │
                         │ IS GREATER THAN      │
START file-name-1 ┌ KEY ┤ IS >                 ├ data-name-1 ┐
                  │      │ IS NOT LESS THAN     │             │
                  │      │ IS NOT <             │             │
                  │      │ IS GREATER THAN OR EQUAL TO        │
                  └      └ IS >=                ┘             ┘
```

```
        ┌ REGARDLESS OF LOCK        ┐
        │                           │
        │            ┌ UPDATERS ┐   │
        │ ALLOWING   ┤ READERS  ├   │
        │            └ NO OTHERS ┘   │
        └                           ┘
```

```
   [INVALID KEY imperative-statement-1]
   [NOT INVALID KEY imperative-statement-2]
   [END-START]
```

```
        ┌ RUN       ┐
STOP    ┤ literal-1 ┘
```

STORE record-name [[NEXT TO] DBKEY] [WITHIN {realm-name} ...]

```
        ┌              ┌┌   REALM              ┐┐             ┐
        │              ││   RECORD             ││             │
        │ RETAINING    ┤│                      ├│ CURRENCY    │
        │              ││ ┌ SET [set-name] ... ┐│             │
        │              ││ └ {set-name} ...     ┘│             │
        └              └└                      ┘┘             ┘
```

STRING $\left\{ \begin{Bmatrix} \text{identifier-1} \\ \text{literal-1} \end{Bmatrix} \dots \text{DELIMITED BY} \begin{Bmatrix} \text{identifier-2} \\ \text{literal-2} \\ \text{SIZE} \end{Bmatrix} \right\} \dots$

    INTO identifier-3
    [WITH POINTER identifier-4]
    [ON OVERFLOW imperative-statement-1]
    [NOT ON OVERFLOW imperative-statement-2]
    [END-STRING]

SUBTRACT $\begin{Bmatrix} \text{identifier-1} \\ \text{literal-1} \end{Bmatrix} \dots$ FROM {identifier-3 [ROUNDED]} ...

    [ON SIZE ERROR imperative-statement-1]
    [NOT ON SIZE ERROR imperative-statement-2]
    [END-SUBTRACT]

SUBTRACT $\begin{Bmatrix} \text{identifier-1} \\ \text{literal-1} \end{Bmatrix} \dots$ FROM $\begin{Bmatrix} \text{identifier-2} \\ \text{literal-2} \end{Bmatrix}$

    GIVING {identifier-3 [ROUNDED]} ...
    [ON SIZE ERROR imperative-statement-1]
    [NOT ON SIZE ERROR imperative-statement-2]
    [END-SUBTRACT]

SUBTRACT $\left\{\begin{array}{l} \underline{\text{CORRESPONDING}} \\ \underline{\text{CORR}} \end{array}\right\}$ identifier-1 FROM identifier-2 [ROUNDED]

    [ON SIZE ERROR imperative-statement-1]
    [NOT ON SIZE ERROR imperative-statement-2]
    [END-SUBTRACT]

SUPPRESS PRINTING

TERMINATE {report-name-1} . . .

UNLOCK file-name $\left[\begin{array}{l} \text{RECORD} \\ \text{ALL RECORDS} \end{array}\right]$

UNSTRING identifier-1

    $\left[\underline{\text{DELIMITED}} \text{ BY } [\underline{\text{ALL}}] \left\{\begin{array}{l} \text{identifier-2} \\ \text{literal-1} \end{array}\right\} \left[\underline{\text{OR}} [\underline{\text{ALL}}] \left\{\begin{array}{l} \text{identifier-3} \\ \text{literal-2} \end{array}\right\} \right] \cdots \right]$

        INTO {identifier-4 [DELIMITER IN identifier-5] [COUNT IN identifier-6]} . . .
        [WITH POINTER identifier-7]
        [TALLYING IN identifier-8]
        [ON OVERFLOW imperative-statement-1]
        [NOT ON OVERFLOW imperative-statement-2]
        [END-UNSTRING]

USE [GLOBAL] AFTER STANDARD $\left\{\begin{array}{l} \text{EXCEPTION} \\ \text{ERROR} \end{array}\right\}$ PROCEDURE ON $\left\{\begin{array}{l} \text{\{file-name-1\} . . .} \\ \text{INPUT} \\ \text{OUTPUT} \\ \text{I-O} \\ \text{EXTEND} \end{array}\right\}$

USE [GLOBAL] AFTER STANDARD $\begin{Bmatrix} \underline{BEGINNING} \\ \underline{END} \end{Bmatrix}$

$\begin{Bmatrix} FILE \\ REEL \\ UNIT \end{Bmatrix}$ LABEL PROCEDURE ON $\begin{Bmatrix} file\text{-}name \\ \underline{INPUT} \\ \underline{OUTPUT} \\ \underline{I\text{-}O} \\ \underline{EXTEND} \end{Bmatrix}$

USE [GLOBAL] BEFORE REPORTING identifier-1

USE FOR DEBUGGING ON $\begin{Bmatrix} cd\text{-}name\text{-}1 \\ [\underline{ALL} \text{ REFERENCES OF}] \text{ identifier-1} \\ file\text{-}name\text{-}1 \\ procedure\text{-}name\text{-}1 \\ \underline{ALL} \underline{PROCEDURES} \end{Bmatrix}$ ...

USE [GLOBAL] FOR DB-EXCEPTION
$\left[ON \begin{Bmatrix} \{DBM\$\_exception\text{-}condition\} \text{ ...} \\ \underline{OTHER} \end{Bmatrix} \right]$

S WRITE record-name-1 [FROM identifier-1]
    [ALLOWING NO OTHERS]

62

$$\left[\left\{\begin{matrix}\underline{\text{BEFORE}}\\\underline{\text{AFTER}}\end{matrix}\right\}\quad\text{ADVANCING}\quad\left\{\begin{matrix}\left\{\begin{matrix}\text{identifier-2}\\\text{integer-1}\end{matrix}\right\}\quad\left[\begin{matrix}\text{LINE}\\\text{LINES}\end{matrix}\right]\\\left\{\begin{matrix}\text{mnemonic-name-1}\\\underline{\text{PAGE}}\end{matrix}\right\}\end{matrix}\right\}\right]$$

$$\left[\text{AT}\quad\left\{\begin{matrix}\underline{\text{END-OF-PAGE}}\\\underline{\text{EOP}}\end{matrix}\right\}\quad\text{imperative-statement-1}\right]$$

$$\left[\underline{\text{NOT}}\,\text{AT}\quad\left\{\begin{matrix}\underline{\text{END-OF-PAGE}}\\\underline{\text{EOP}}\end{matrix}\right\}\quad\text{imperative-statement-2}\right]$$

$$[\text{END-WRITE}]$$

RI <u>WRITE</u> record-name-1 [<u>FROM</u> identifier-1]

[<u>ALLOWING</u> <u>NO</u> OTHERS]

[<u>INVALID</u> KEY imperative-statement-1]

[<u>NOT</u> <u>INVALID</u> KEY imperative-statement-2]

[END-WRITE]

General Format for Copy and Replace Statements

<u>COPY</u> text-name-1 $\left[\left\{\begin{matrix}\underline{\text{OF}}\\\underline{\text{IN}}\end{matrix}\right\}\text{ library-name-1}\right]$

$$\left[\; \underline{\text{REPLACING}}\; \left\{\begin{array}{l} ==\text{pseudo-text-1}== \\ \text{identifier-1} \\ \text{literal-1} \\ \text{word-1} \end{array}\right\} \; \underline{\text{BY}}\; \left\{\begin{array}{l} ==\text{pseudo-text-2}== \\ \text{identifier-2} \\ \text{literal-2} \\ \text{word-2} \end{array}\right\} \right] \ldots \;\right]$$

$\underline{\text{COPY}}$ record-name $\underline{\text{FROM}}$ $\underline{\text{DICTIONARY}}$

$$\left[\begin{array}{l} \underline{\text{REPLACING}} \\ \left\{\left\{\begin{array}{l} ==\text{pseudo-text-1}== \\ \text{identifier-1} \\ \text{literal-1} \\ \text{word-1} \end{array}\right\} \; \underline{\text{BY}}\; \left\{\begin{array}{l} ==\text{pseudo-text-2}== \\ \text{identifier-2} \\ \text{literal-2} \\ \text{word-2} \end{array}\right\}\right\} \ldots \end{array}\right].$$

$\underline{\text{REPLACE}}$ {==pseudo-text-1== BY ==pseudo-text-2==} ...
$\underline{\text{REPLACE}}$ $\underline{\text{OFF}}$

General Format for Conditions

RELATION CONDITION

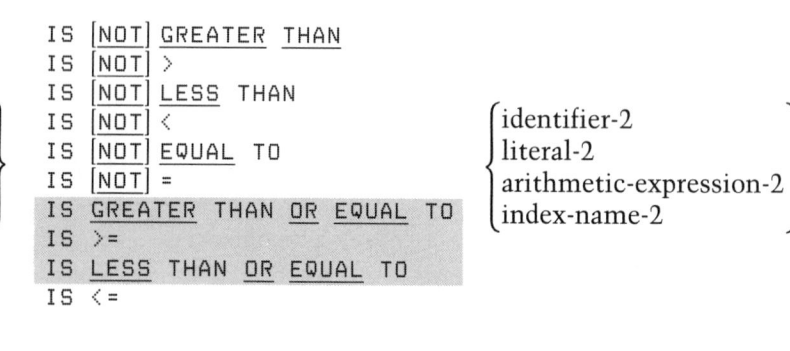

```
            IS [NOT] GREATER THAN
            IS [NOT] >
            IS [NOT] LESS THAN
⎧identifier-1           ⎫   IS [NOT] <           ⎧identifier-2           ⎫
⎪literal-1              ⎪   IS [NOT] EQUAL TO    ⎪literal-2              ⎪
⎨arithmetic-expression-1⎬   IS [NOT] =           ⎨arithmetic-expression-2⎬
⎪index-name-1           ⎪   IS GREATER THAN OR EQUAL TO  ⎪index-name-2    ⎪
⎩                       ⎭   IS >=                ⎩                       ⎭
                            IS LESS THAN OR EQUAL TO
                            IS <=
```

CLASS CONDITION

```
                     ⎧NUMERIC          ⎫
                     ⎪ALPHABETIC       ⎪
identifier-1 IS [NOT]⎨ALPHABETIC-LOWER ⎬
                     ⎪ALPHABETIC-UPPER ⎪
                     ⎩class-name       ⎭
```

CONDITION-NAME CONDITION

condition-name-1

$$\underline{CURRENT} \left[\text{WITHIN} \begin{Bmatrix} \text{record-name} \\ \text{set-name} \\ \text{realm-name} \end{Bmatrix} \right]$$

KEEPLIST ACCESS

$$\begin{Bmatrix} \underline{OFFSET} & \text{integer-exp} \\ \underline{FIRST} \\ \underline{LAST} \end{Bmatrix} \quad \underline{WITHIN} \text{ keeplist-name}$$

SWITCH-STATUS CONDITION

condition-name-1

SIGN CONDITION

$$\text{arithmetic-expression-1} \quad \underline{IS} \; [\underline{NOT}] \begin{Bmatrix} \underline{POSITIVE} \\ \underline{NEGATIVE} \\ \underline{ZERO} \end{Bmatrix}$$

TENANCY CONDITION

$$[\underline{NOT}] \; [\text{set-name}] \begin{Bmatrix} \underline{OWNER} \\ \underline{MEMBER} \\ \underline{TENANT} \end{Bmatrix}$$

DATABASE KEY CONDITION

$$\text{database-key} \quad \underline{IS} \; [\underline{NOT}] \begin{Bmatrix} \underline{ALSO} & \text{database-key} \\ \underline{NULL} \\ \underline{WITHIN} & \text{keeplist-name} \end{Bmatrix}$$

66

SUCCESS/FAILURE CONDITION

status-code-id IS $\left\{ \begin{array}{c} \underline{SUCCESS} \\ \underline{FAILURE} \end{array} \right\}$

NEGATED CONDITION

<u>NOT</u> condition-1

COMBINED CONDITION

condition-1 $\left\{ \left\{ \begin{array}{c} \underline{AND} \\ \underline{OR} \end{array} \right\} \text{condition-2} \right\} \ldots$

ABBREVIATED COMBINED RELATION CONDITION

relation-condition $\left\{ \left\{ \begin{array}{c} \underline{AND} \\ \underline{OR} \end{array} \right\} [\underline{NOT}] \text{ [relational-operator] object} \right\} \ldots$

DATABASE KEY IDENTIFIER ACCESS

database-key-identifier

DATABASE SET OWNER ACCESS

<u>OWNER</u> WITHIN set-name

RECORD SEARCH ACCESS

$$\left\{ \begin{array}{l} \underline{FIRST} \\ \underline{LAST} \\ \underline{NEXT} \\ \underline{PRIOR} \\ \underline{ANY} \\ \underline{DUPLICATE} \\ [\underline{RELATIVE}] \quad \text{int-exp} \end{array} \right\}$$

[record-name] $\left[\underline{WITHIN} \left\{ \begin{array}{l} \text{realm-name} \\ \text{set-name} \end{array} \right\} \right] \left[\begin{array}{l} \underline{USING} \; [\text{record-key}] \ldots \\ \underline{WHERE} \; [\text{boolean-expression}] \end{array} \right]$

boolean-express:
{boolean-alt   [$\underline{OR}$ boolean-alt] . . .}

boolean-alt:
{simple-boolean-relation   [$\underline{AND}$ simple-boolean-relation] . . .}

simple-boolean-relation:
$\left\{ \begin{array}{l} \text{boolean-condition} \\ \underline{NOT} \;\; \text{boolean-expression} \end{array} \right\}$

boolean-condition:

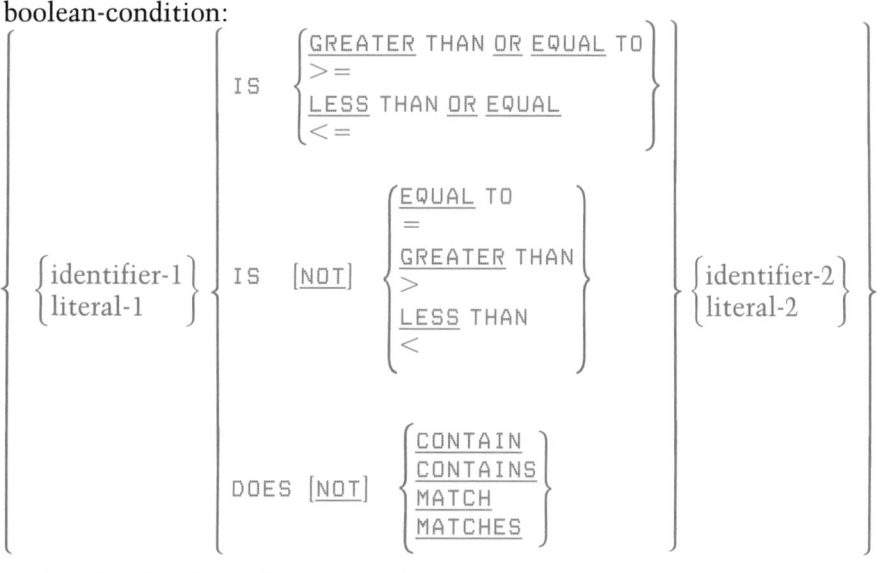

DATABASE ON ERROR CONDITION

[NOT] ON ERROR imperative statement

RETAINING CLAUSE

$$
\left[\text{RETAINING} \left[\left\{\left|\begin{array}{l}\underline{\text{REALM}} \\ \underline{\text{RECORD}} \\ \left\{\begin{array}{l}\underline{\text{SET}}\ [\text{set-name}]\ \dots \\ \{\text{set-name}\}\ \dots\end{array}\right\}\end{array}\right|\right\}\right] \text{CURRENCY}\right]
$$

Qualification

FORMAT 1

$$
\left\{\begin{array}{l}\text{data-name-1} \\ \text{condition-name}\end{array}\right\} \left\{\begin{array}{l}\left\{\left\{\begin{array}{l}\underline{\text{IN}} \\ \underline{\text{OF}}\end{array}\right\} \text{data-name-2}\right\} \dots \left[\left\{\begin{array}{l}\underline{\text{IN}} \\ \underline{\text{OF}}\end{array}\right\} \left\{\begin{array}{l}\text{file-name} \\ \text{cd-name}\end{array}\right\}\right] \\ \left\{\begin{array}{l}\underline{\text{IN}} \\ \underline{\text{OF}}\end{array}\right\} \left\{\begin{array}{l}\text{file-name} \\ \text{cd-name}\end{array}\right\}\end{array}\right\}
$$

FORMAT 2

$$
\text{paragraph-name} \left\{\begin{array}{l}\underline{\text{IN}} \\ \underline{\text{OF}}\end{array}\right\} \text{section-name}
$$

FORMAT 3

$$
\text{text-name} \left\{\begin{array}{l}\underline{\text{IN}} \\ \underline{\text{OF}}\end{array}\right\} \text{library-name}
$$

70

FORMAT 4

$$\underline{\text{LINAGE-COUNTER}} \quad \left\{ \begin{matrix} \underline{\text{IN}} \\ \underline{\text{OF}} \end{matrix} \right\} \quad \text{report-name}$$

FORMAT 5

$$\left\{ \begin{matrix} \underline{\text{PAGE-COUNTER}} \\ \underline{\text{LINE-COUNTER}} \end{matrix} \right\} \quad \left\{ \begin{matrix} \underline{\text{IN}} \\ \underline{\text{OF}} \end{matrix} \right\} \quad \text{report-name}$$

FORMAT 6

$$\text{data-name-3} \quad \left\{ \begin{matrix} \left\{ \begin{matrix} \underline{\text{IN}} \\ \underline{\text{OF}} \end{matrix} \right\} \text{data-name-4} \quad \left[\left\{ \begin{matrix} \underline{\text{IN}} \\ \underline{\text{OF}} \end{matrix} \right\} \text{report-name} \right] \\ \left\{ \begin{matrix} \underline{\text{IN}} \\ \underline{\text{OF}} \end{matrix} \right\} \text{report-name} \end{matrix} \right\}$$

Miscellaneous Formats

SUBSCRIPTING

$$\left\{ \begin{matrix} \text{condition-name-1} \\ \text{data-name-1} \end{matrix} \right\} \quad (\left\{ \begin{matrix} \text{integer-1} \\ \text{data-name-2} \ [\{\pm\} \ \text{integer-2}] \\ \text{index-name-1} \ [\{\pm\} \ \text{integer-3}] \\ \text{arithmetic-expression} \end{matrix} \right\} \cdots)$$

REFERENCE MODIFICATION

data-name-1 (leftmost-character-position: [length])

IDENTIFIER

data-name-1 $\left[\left\{ \begin{matrix} IN \\ OF \end{matrix} \right\} \text{data-name-2} \right]$ ... $\left[\left\{ \begin{matrix} IN \\ OF \end{matrix} \right\} \left\{ \begin{matrix} \text{cd-name} \\ \text{file-name} \\ \text{report-name} \end{matrix} \right\} \right]$

[({subscript} ...)]   [(leftmost-character-position: [length])]

General Format for Nested Source Programs

```
IDENTIFICATION DIVISION.
PROGRAM-ID.  program-name-1 [IS INITIAL PROGRAM].
[ENVIRONMENT DIVISION.  environment-division-content]
[DATA DIVISION.  data-division-content]
[PROCEDURE DIVISION.  procedure-division-content]
[[nested-source-program] ...
END PROGRAM program-name-1.]
```

72

![General Format for Nested-Source-Program]

General Format for Nested-Source-Program

<u>IDENTIFICATION</u> <u>DIVISION</u>.

<u>PROGRAM-ID</u>.   program-name-2 $\left[\text{IS} \left\{ \left| \begin{array}{c} \underline{\text{COMMON}} \\ \underline{\text{INITIAL}} \end{array} \right| \right\} \text{PROGRAM} \right]$.

[<u>ENVIRONMENT</u> <u>DIVISION</u>.   environment-division-content]
[<u>DATA</u> <u>DIVISION</u>.   data-division-content]
[<u>PROCEDURE</u> <u>DIVISION</u>.   procedure-division-content]
[nested-source-program] . . .
<u>END</u> <u>PROGRAM</u> program-name-2.

General Format for a Sequence of Source Programs

{<u>IDENTIFICATION</u> <u>DIVISION</u>.
 <u>PROGRAM-ID</u>.   program-name-3 [IS <u>INITIAL</u> PROGRAM].
[<u>ENVIRONMENT</u> <u>DIVISION</u>.   environment-division-content]
[<u>DATA</u> <u>DIVISION</u>.   data-division-content]
[<u>PROCEDURE</u> <u>DIVISION</u>.   procedure-division-content]
[nested-source-program] . . .
 <u>END</u> <u>PROGRAM</u> program-name-3.} . . .
 <u>IDENTIFICATION</u> <u>DIVISION</u>.
 <u>PROGRAM-ID</u>.   program-name-4 [IS <u>INITIAL</u> PROGRAM].
[<u>ENVIRONMENT</u> <u>DIVISION</u>.   environment-division-content]

[DATA DIVISION. data-division-content]
[PROCEDURE DIVISION. procedure-division-content]
[[nested-source-program] . . .
END PROGRAM program-name-4.]